Vietnam 1965–68

US Air Cavalry Trooper

VERSUS

North Vietnamese Soldier

Chris McNab

Illustrated by Johnny Shumate

OSPREY PUBLISHING
Bloomsbury Publishing Plc
Kemp House, Chawley Park, Cumnor Hill, Oxford OX2 9PH, UK
1385 Broadway, 5th Floor, New York, NY 10018, USA
E-mail: info@ospreypublishing.com
www.ospreypublishing.com

OSPREY is a trademark of Osprey Publishing Ltd

First published in Great Britain in 2020

A catalog record for this book is available from the British Library.

ISBN: PB 9781472841759; eBook 9781472841766;
ePDF 9781472841735; XML 9781472841742

20 21 22 23 24   10 9 8 7 6 5 4 3 2 1

Index by Rob Munro
Typeset by PDQ Digital Media Solutions, Bungay, UK
Printed and bound in India by Replika Press Private Ltd.

Osprey Publishing supports the Woodland Trust, the UK's leading woodland conservation charity.

To find out more about our authors and books visit
www.ospreypublishing.com. Here you will find extracts, author interviews, details of forthcoming events and the option to sign up for our newsletter.

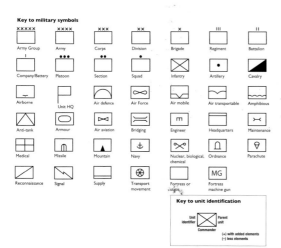

Acknowledgments

Special thanks go to Richard Dieterle, Vietnam Air Cavalry veteran, for his thoughtful and constructive read-through of my text (any mistakes are purely my own, however) and for his permission to use an extract from his combat account "The Firefight at Dai Dong." The full text of this account, plus many other fascinating veteran narratives, can be found at https://vnwarstories.com/

CONTENTS

Introduction

In a US Army November 1965 publication entitled *The Airmobile Division*, the writers describe both the composition and the potential of the new 1st Cavalry Division (Airmobile), formed just months earlier:

> The stillness of the jungle is suddenly shattered by the sounds of approaching helicopters, flying just above the treetops. Caught by surprise in their hidden rest area, the guerrillas begin to seek even more concealment. They hear machineguns and air-to-ground rockets firing and realize that the armed helicopters are laying down suppressive fire. This fact tells them that fresh, ready-to-fight, troops soon will be coming to earth all around their position. They realize that the thing all guerillas fear – encirclement – is about to occur. (US Army 1965: 10)

Unlike many official military publications of the time, this one features a dramatic artwork on the cover, showing a UH-1 helicopter in a steep and aggressive descent, unleashing firepower as it does so from its side-mounted rocket pods. Matching the spirit of the artwork, the quoted text above, sitting among far drier passages of technical and organizational information, forms part of a stirring narrative envisioning how the division and its tactics might change the face of warfare itself.

The sight and sound of helicopters in the Vietnam War (1963–75), most notably the ubiquitous UH-1, have become such popular signatures of the conflict that we can easily forget just how *new* helicopter airmobility was at this time. Small numbers of helicopters had been used by the US Army during the Korean War (1950–53), principally for light supply, medevac, and reconnaissance duties, but although some farsighted individuals understood the need for a greater airmobility in the future, the concept needed a jump-start if it was to take hold.

The starting pistol was fired in the April 1954 edition of *Harper's Magazine*, via an article penned by Major General James M. Gavin, commander of the

82d Airborne Division during World War II and a noted postwar tactical thinker. In the article – entitled "Cavalry, and I Don't Mean Horses!" – Gavin argued that the strong emphasis on tanks had taken hold of the cavalry concept, disastrously so (Gavin 1954). Faced with new enemies and tactics, however, the very understanding of cavalry needed a technological and tactical renewal. Gavin explained that as the modern enemy was now typically dispersed in the defense, it was imperative for units conducting offensive actions to concentrate rapidly and simultaneously at locations from which offensive forces could seize the maneuver advantage. To do so, they required the capability to deploy, resupply, and reinforce at distance from home bases to enable them to seize tactical advantages. He went on to argue that the means of this mobility was now truly available, in the form of helicopters and transport/utility aircraft.

Gavin's article, which coincided with the progressing emergence of better, more capable helicopter types, triggered several important experimental tests of the "Sky-Cav" concept, plus further impetus behind the development of US Army fixed- and rotary-wing aviation. Proposals for an airmobile division were also on the drawing board by 1958.

One of the most significant advances toward airmobility was the formation in early 1960 of the Army Aircraft Requirements Review Board (the Rogers Board, named after its chairman, Lieutenant General Gordon B. Rogers), which gave focus to the development of specific new aircraft types, including the HU-1 utility helicopter that would become the backbone of the 1st Cavalry Division (Airmobile), plus the HC-1 Chinook heavy-lift helicopter. (A 1962 redesignation program saw the HU-1 – a designation which had given rise to the Iroquois' familiar nickname of "Huey" – become the UH-1 and the HC-1 the CH-47.) The second was the conclusions of the Army Tactical Requirements Board (the Howze Board, named after Lieutenant General Hamilton H. Howze), which submitted a report in

August 1962 that explicitly recommended the establishment of air assault divisions and air cavalry combat brigades. (The board had been formed at the pressing request of Secretary of Defense Robert S. McNamara, a governmental advocate of the airmobile concept.) These major formations would have full airlift capability through organic air assets, having only about one-third of the land vehicles of a traditional infantry division. Tactically, they would use this trans-dimensional mobility to revolutionize the reach, flexibility, and speed of assault operations.

Despite resistance from many quarters – not least the US Air Force, jealously guarding its aerial remit – the airmobile concept received the funding and effort required to allow it to become a reality. In 1963 the 11th Air Assault Division (Test) and 10th Air Transport Brigade were activated to give shape to airmobility, and led directly to the establishment of the 1st Cavalry Division (Airmobile) on June 15, 1965. Alongside organic aviation units developed within other US Army formations, the division gave the US Army a new type of sword to wield in a new type of war, a conflict that was expanding in South Vietnam with every passing month.

The North Vietnamese soldiers of the PAVN (People's Army of Vietnam; *Quan Doi Dang Dan*) who would confront the 1st Cavalry Division (Airmobile) between 1965 and 1972 could scarcely have presented a greater contrast with the US forces. For the soldiers of the PAVN, airmobility would forever be beyond their reach. Instead, they deployed to the battlefields sometimes in trucks and light vehicles (if they were lucky), but mostly on foot and bicycles. They fought their attackers from the sky with the basic tools of infantry warfare: small arms, grenades, mortars, and light artillery. The US airborne warriors wielded immense destructive force even before infantry boots touched the ground, in the form of helicopter weapon systems, the bombs and cannon of supporting fixed-wing aviation, plus long-range artillery. Yet, as the battles of this book demonstrate, this did not result in a straightforward superiority of US over PAVN forces. The US troops would, at least tactically, always triumph, but the intelligence, aggression, and resilience of the PAVN soldier ensured that these victories came at a sobering cost.

Key to PAVN forces' survival when faced with US search-and-destroy tactics was fast movement. Here a PAVN/VC force move through jungle terrain in classic fire-and-maneuver bounds, the soldier in the foreground providing cover as the others sprint forward. (Keystone/Hulton archive/Getty Images)

Infiltration into Binh Dinh Province, 1965–67

Binh Dinh Province was in the far northeast of II Corps Tactical Zone. Much of this province is mountainous in nature, particularly in the north and west, but it also has a long coastline. The province was heavily infiltrated by both PAVN units and also VC (Viet Cong) forces from neighboring provinces. The rough lines of the principal infiltration routes and the general areas of concentration (the pale-red circles) are marked here, but there would have been considerable variation and adaptation depending on the nature of the objectives and the responses to American and ARVN actions. In the lower half of the map, we can see the 1st Air Cav's main base at An Khe.

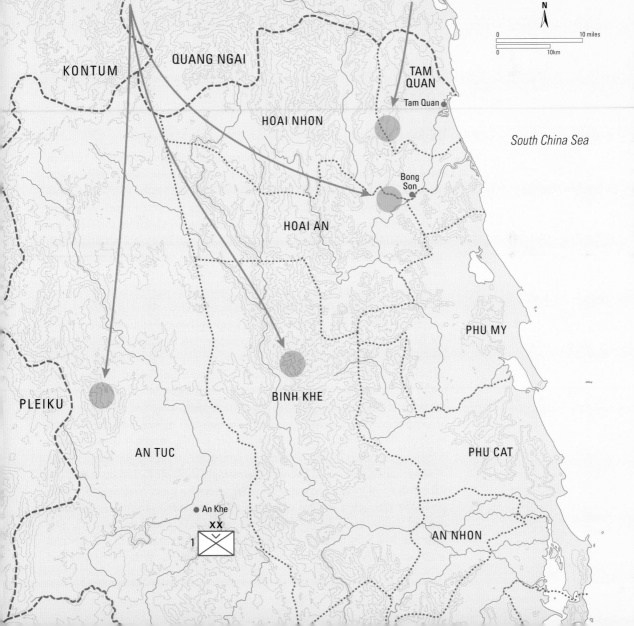

KONTUM

QUANG NGAI

TAM QUAN

Tam Quan

HOAI NHON

South China Sea

Bong Son

HOAI AN

PHU MY

PLEIKU

BINH KHE

AN TUC

PHU CAT

An Khe

XX

1

AN NHON

N

0   10 miles
0   10km

The Opposing Sides

COMMAND AND CONTROL

US Air Cav

The Air Cav employed the standard hierarchical models of command used in the wider US Army. The chief difference lay in its composition and tactical purpose. The 1st Cavalry Division (Airmobile) – the 1st Air Cav – was a true combined-arms formation, with organic logistics, troop transport, air power, artillery, reconnaissance, engineer, and other elements all within the divisional package, which was designed largely for flexible and unilateral action. (Many operations, however, did involve non-divisional assets working in support, such as additional aviation companies.)

In terms of Air Cav command and control during combat operations, the big challenge was for a battalion commander to retain a sense and an awareness of what was going on over a large and complex area of operations (AO), with the multiplicity of assets requiring an intricate choreography if chaos was to be avoided. Command and control was therefore also a fully airmobile asset, with the operation commander and other leaders (who could be at battalion, regiment, brigade, or division levels, depending on the scale of the mission) circling the battlefield in scout helicopters, usually accompanied by an assistant, the S3 (Operations) officer, and artillery and aviation liaison officers. The commander would receive real-time radio communications from the various unit commanders on the ground, a stream of information that could become increasingly difficult to process under the data rush of an evolving combat situation. Ground units could identify their positions through a variety of means: radio encoded ground coordinates, colored smoke grenades and flares, marker panels, and signal mirrors. The commander's assistant could therefore plot the positions of both friendly and enemy troops on a mapboard. Using this information, all the assets involved

in the operation – artillery, helicopter gunships, scout helicopters, close air support (CAS), resupply, medevac, etc. – could be coordinated from the aerial command point, making command and control capable of responding very rapidly to the evolving situation (Rottman 2009). Scout helicopters (typically types such as the Bell OH-13 Sioux, Hughes OH-6A Cayuse, and Hiller OH-23 Raven) also had a crucial role within the command-and-control framework, by making overflights of landing zones (LZs) and the surrounding area to spot enemy activity, often by virtue of the fact that they attracted ground fire. The scout helicopters would relay their findings to the commander or to accompanying helicopter gunships, which could deliver immediate suppression if required.

Electronic communications were naturally critical to efficient airmobile command and control. Two pieces of radio technology were central between 1965 and 1968: the AN/VRC-12 and AN/PRC-25 radio sets, the latter of which General William C. Westmoreland, commander of Military Assistance Command, Vietnam (MACV) from June 1964 through June 1968, referred to as one of the most important tactical tools in Vietnam. The AN/VRC-12 was a tactical vehicular radio set and provided 920 VHF/FM voice channels in the 30–76MHz range. It was typically installed in divisional and brigade command posts or, in the airmobile context, aboard command helicopters. Each of these helicopters would have two or even three of the sets aboard, the preset channel functions on the radios meaning that the commander could switch between multiple net levels quickly, from brigade communications down to front-line battalions and companies.

Down on the ground, it was the AN/PRC-25 that did most of the electronic communications work amongst the front-line infantry companies. The set had had 920 channels operating in the 30–75.95MHz spectrum, transmitting with 1.5 watts of power over distances of 5–11km (3–7 miles) with the standard antenna, depending on the terrain and other factors. The radio set was conveniently supported with a web suspender rig or mounted on the LC-2 pack frame from the All-Purpose Lightweight Individual Carrying Equipment (ALICE) pack. The AN/PRC-25 was progressively replaced with the improved AN/PRC-77 from 1968 onward. Being a radioman was a

ABOVE LEFT
UH-1 helicopters of the 1st Cavalry Division (Airmobile) on approach to landing in January 1966, the dust whipped up from their rotor blades obscuring the sky. Loose stones at a landing site could become genuinely dangerous missiles under the blast of rotor downwash. (Photo by Co Rentmeester/ The LIFE Picture Collection via Getty Images)

ABOVE RIGHT
A US 1st Air Cav soldier leads away a VC suspect during Operation *Irving* in October 1966. Note the handset mounted on the soldier's chest, connecting to the AN/ PRC-25 radio on his back. This radio set was an advanced solid-state design, far lighter than the previous AN/PRC-10. (Bettmann via Getty Images)

This US soldier is typical of the troops of the 1st Cavalry Division (Airmobile) as they would have appeared in the period 1966–68. He is part of the fighting around Tam Quan in 1967, moving forward in the assault on Dai Dong on December 8. He is relatively new to Vietnam, having recently arrived as a replacement. New recruits would go for one week's in-country orientation with the First Team Academy at Bien Hoa, before being sent to the operational unit.

Weapons, dress, and equipment

The soldier is armed with the XM16E1 assault rifle (**1**), which weighed 6.5lb and measured 39.5in. It was an improved version of the original M16 assault rifle, and featured (on some weapons) a closed, "bird-cage" flash suppressor (although prong-type suppressors were still common) and, most important, a forward-assist device (on the top right-side of the receiver), which enabled the soldier to physically check that the bolt was properly locked in battery before firing. He also carries two types of grenade: the M26A1 fragmentation (**2**) grenade for antipersonnel use, and the M18 Smoke Grenade (obscured from view) for signaling purposes.

His basic uniform consists of the tropical jungle shirt (**3**), with the 1st Air Cav patch on its left upper arm, and matching trousers (**4**). The jacket, which has the third-pattern concealed buttons and angled pockets, was made from all-cotton wind-resistant poplin or rip-stop cotton and was dyed olive-green Army shade 107; the trousers were dyed in the same color, and featured concealed buttons. Although the trousers were light and comfortable for the tropical climate, they had a tendency to tear at the knee. His footwear (**5**) is the canvas-and-leather combination jungle boots, a big improvement over the all-leather boots that US soldiers

wore at the beginning of the Vietnam War. The canvas sections gave the wearer's feet welcome ventilation, to help them dry out when wet, while the Vibram rubber sole delivered a degree of nonslip traction. For head protection, the soldier has the classic M1 steel helmet (**6**) with improved chinstrap and camouflage cover and rubber utility band. The cover was reversible: green for jungle and wet season green vegetation, and tan for dry season yellow grass.

The soldier is heavily laden with equipment, which is suspended on the M1956 Load-Carrying Equipment (**7**). Items supported by the webbing system include ammunition pouches for his rifle (**8**), a dressing/medical case which contained an atropine injector (**9**), two plastic 1-quart water canteens with M1956 covers (**10**; the cover had a synthetic-wool felt lining for insulation), the M1956 field pack (**11**), an M17 Protective Mask (**12**) – essential when the US forces were using CS (tear) gas or other irritants in the area – and a rolled-up poncho (**13**), one of which was usually carried between two men. A veteran informed the author that about half the gas masks failed because their owner failed to carry them on top of their helmets when crossing streams.

critical but dangerous role in battlefield command and control, as the enemy forces would naturally target such important individuals in firefights.

For the airmobile infantry, the battalion was the key maneuver element, divided into infantry companies, platoons, and squads (see page 78 for more details), plus various support platoons. In the confined and fragmented landscape that was characteristic of much of Vietnam, small-unit leadership was often the critical factor in engagements; a regional operation could quickly devolve into a tapestry of platoon and squad contacts. A rifle platoon was led by a lieutenant, who had under his control three squads, each of roughly 6–13 men. The lieutenant's platoon headquarters consisted of the lieutenant himself, a platoon sergeant, and a radio operator; the latter was vital in enabling the platoon to orientate itself in relation to the other US units around it, and the movement of air assets into and out of the LZs and medevac areas. The lieutenants and the platoon's NCOs also had to be flexible in their command processes, as the realities of combat and casualties often meant that they went into action with manpower significantly below that established in the table of organization and equipment (TO&E.)

PAVN

When considering the organization of the PAVN, we must avoid popular misconceptions. In this book, when it comes to communist forces our principal focus is on the PAVN, the conventional army of North Vietnam. At times we also include the indigenous South Vietnamese insurgency force known as the National Front for the Liberation of South Vietnam (*Mat tran Dan toc Giai phong mien Nam Viet Nam*), or National Liberation Front (NLF) – also known as the "Viet Cong" – but only their "Main Force" units, which mirrored the PAVN in structure, weapons, and tactics, and which came under direct authority of the PAVN. That shorthand label Viet Cong (VC; *Dang Viet Nam Cong San* or Vietnamese Communist Party) is occasionally and incorrectly applied as a blanket term for all communist troops fighting in South Vietnam, whatever their nature or purpose. In reality the VC and PAVN were very different organizations below the Main Force elements, and at times did not coexist in a particularly cooperative relationship. We must also be clear that between 1963 and just prior to the Tet Offensive in January 1968, it was the VC who posed the largest overall combat threat to Army of the Republic of Vietnam (ARVN) and US forces, although the balance of that relationship would progressively shift in favor of the PAVN. In July 1965, US intelligence estimates put the total number of PAVN troops in South Vietnam (i.e. those North Vietnamese troops sent south of the border, not the total number of personnel in the PAVN) at just 7,500, as opposed to 245,000 VC operatives. By 1968 the PAVN strength had risen to about 55,000, but that figure was still dwarfed by the Viet Cong.

All PAVN military activity was rationalized geographically in a system of Military Regions (MR; *quan khu*): North Vietnam itself had regions 1–4, while South Vietnam was carved into regions 5–9. The two regions most important for our analysis were MR 5 and MR 6, which essentially covered the ARVN's I and II Corps Tactical Zones (CTZs) and the northern provinces of III CTZ.

The PAVN unit structures and command and control were those of a conventional army, but had an emphasis on flexibility, either through deliberate organizational choice or *in extremis* rearrangement to reflect the combat situation or battlefield losses. For combat operations in the South, PAVN units were typically arranged into "fronts" for command-and-control purposes, working directly off orders from Hanoi or sometimes through the VC's Central Officer for South Vietnam (COSVN). These fronts were highly mutable entities, not always equating to the corps-size strength associated with the classic Soviet Army formations. They were purposely designed around the operational goals at hand, hence were variable in their composition according to the objectives, the length of the campaign, the assets available, and many other variables. A command structure would be designed around these variables, but a PAVN division in the field always had a normal headquarters company overseeing operations.

Generally speaking, the PAVN attempted to follow a "rule of three" principle, each unit being divided into three subunits, right down to the lowest form of front-line command structure, the "three-man cell," three of which formed a squad. (See page 78 for more information on the structure of PAVN units.) The cells had both utility and combat functions. In combat, an individual cell would often have an identity based on its principal weapon type, e.g. a light machine gun or RPG-2 or RPG-7 grenade launchers (Rottman 2009). If a weapon was particularly demanding in terms of requisite manpower – e.g. a heavy mortar or cannon – the duties to operate it might be divided between more than one cell. Back at base, the cell would function as a work unit with specific tasks. The three-man cell was a useful entity both in terms of tactics and morale, forming a kind of tripartite "buddy" system as practiced by many modern armies.

North Vietnamese military structures were always mirrored by political authority – the PAVN had to ensure that its officers and men were ideologically aligned as well as militarily governed. Military and political commands influenced all levels of the organizational hierarchy, mirroring methods pioneered by the Chinese communists. Dual command structures would be established for major operations, with the headquarters for both typically based just across the border in North Vietnam, Laos, or Cambodia. Political

ABOVE LEFT
PAVN recruits form up on the streets of Hanoi, having volunteered for military service, although conscription was the main source of manpower. Not all PAVN soldiers found themselves fighting in South Vietnam; many, for example, were redirected to labor battalions in North Vietnam. (Sovfoto/ Universal Images Group via Getty Images)

ABOVE RIGHT
Women were primarily recruited into the ranks of the PAVN and VC in support roles, their duties ranging from cooking and nursing through to transportation and construction. Many found themselves on the front lines, with the result that the division between rear-echelon soldier and combatant becoming very blurred. (Keystone-France\Gamma-Rapho via Getty Images)

This PAVN soldier illustrates the basic nature of uniform and equipment within the North Vietnamese military during the 1960s, when compared to the heavily laden and technologically sophisticated Americans. He is typical of the soldiers who would fight against the US troops during the two-week battle of Tam Quan (December 6–20, 1967), although his appearance is representative of any of the actions described in this book. We see him in the middle of a magazine change during a firefight in the hamlet of Dai Dong.

Weapons, dress, and equipment

The soldier is armed with the RPD light machine gun (**1**), of Soviet origin, although the bulk of PAVN troops would actually be equipped with the Chinese Type 56 copy of the AK-47 assault rifle. The RPD weighed 16.3lb when empty and had an overall length of 40.8in, and it was fed from a 100-round segmented belt stored in a drum container. A spare drum is carried in a Soviet-style canvas ammunition bag on his hip (**2**).

His uniform is the basic green army shirt (**3**) and trousers (**4**). By 1966 the color shades of the uniform could vary considerably, from khaki tan to olive-drab green, but washing and campaign use tended to bleach much of the color out of the fabric. His footwear (**5**) is the canvas and rubber "tennis shoe" type, issued

by the PAVN as a form of jungle combat boot. These shoes were not hardwearing, however, and tended to disintegrate through operational use, especially during the journey down from North Vietnam into South Vietnam, which is why locally produced sandals, their soles cut from used truck tires and held on by inner-tube straps, were the preferred option. His headwear is the popular green "boonie"-style soft hat (**6**), with a chinstrap. Soldiers might also wear the standard PAVN pith helmet made from phenolic, a plastic-impregnated cardboard. The pith helmet generally came in a tan color before 1969, and often featured a camouflaged cover. Other equipment might be hung on the equipment belt (**7**).

control permeated down to the lowest levels of authority. Each company, for example, would have a political officer, typically a senior lieutenant. These officers would conduct the "self-criticism sessions" so integral to PAVN personnel management, encouraging soldiers to speak about their military, emotional, and ideological failings, and to suggest corrective actions. A 1966 RAND Corporation report, based on interviews with VC and PAVN prisoners conducted in 1965, explains how they were conducted:

> Complementary to the three-man cell are other sessions in which the soldier is first criticized by his fellows and is then expected to criticize himself. The sessions, which take place very frequently (and are also practiced within the three-man cell, so that the two systems overlap), seek to bring out all that troubles a man about himself or his comrades. Evidently, inferiors are free to criticize superiors, at least within limits: privates do criticize non-coms, for example, though the net flow of criticism seems to go from higher to lower ranks, and from party members to non-party members. Such sessions apparently provide an emotional catharsis in that they serve to release undesirable tensions or to prevent them from even arising. They are also useful in building up other tensions that can be mobilized and employed by the leaders. In short, they provide a kind of group therapy, Communist style. (Kellen 1966: 36)

In terms of practical battlefield command and control, there were some distinct differences between the US and PAVN forces, not least the levels of reliance upon electronic communications, which were much lower in the PAVN units. US intelligence agencies estimated that whereas personnel with some responsibility for signals/communications could account for up to 20 percent of front-line strength in US forces, that figure dropped to about 5 percent in the PAVN. In 1965, there were no radios at PAVN platoon level and not always radios at company level. Most of the radios and field telephones were held at battalion and regimental levels and were distributed according to perceived need. Regarding the actual types of radio used, these were primarily of Chinese manufacture. There were many models in use, but one of the most common was the Type 102E, which was actually modeled on the US AN/GRC-9, although the Chinese version was bulkier and heavier – the total weight was 105lb.

The relative paucity of radio communications and electronic signaling in PAVN units was partly due to the fact that North Vietnam did not have the wealth of the United States to allow it to invest in communications equipment without restriction. There were also tactical reasons, however. US intelligence personnel were adept at intercepting PAVN radio transmissions, so on many occasions maintaining radio silence was a sound option. Instead, the PAVN developed some more primitive, but still functional, command-and-control techniques. They relied on runners physically taking messages between the platoons and companies and the higher command levels. They also used flares, signal fires, flags, lights, beacons, whistles, and even gunshots (firing a specific number of rounds at understood intervals) to communicate orders and information. Needless to say, the limitations on PAVN command and control had an impact on tactical flexibility, hence the PAVN units relied heavily on pre-combat orders to direct the units once battle had begun.

WEAPONS

US Air Cav

The Americans, free from many of the "manportability" considerations that hung over their North Vietnamese enemy, had few limitations on their firepower. Indeed, the disparity between US firepower (including weaponry supplied to the ARVN) and that of their opponents could not have been more profound. In this book we are focusing specifically on the 1st Air Cav, but we should always see this division within the context of the totality of US force options. Thus as well the formidable weaponry organic to the division, Air Cav operations would also be supported by the firepower of other US infantry and mechanized divisions (the latter bolstered by armored support), plus the astonishing destructive capabilities of US air power. Much like the Japanese during World War II, the soldiers of the PAVN had to adjust to the reality that they could rarely win an engagement based on a head-on attempt to achieve fire superiority.

At the lighter end of the scale of heavy firepower, support weapons used by the Air Cav included the 106mm M40A1 recoilless rifle and the 81mm M29A1 mortar. Weight restrictions imposed upon airmobile operations, however, meant that only limited ammunition for these weapons could be carried by the infantry. Therefore, much of the fire support was provided by the Air Cav's own artillery assets, mainly 105mm M101A1 and 155mm M114 howitzers, which could be transported to forward artillery Fire Support Bases (FSBs) as an underslung load beneath a CH-21B Shawnee, CH-37B/C Mojave, CH-47A Chinook, or CH-54A Tarhe helicopter.

Of course, the other source of fire support came from the weapons mounted on combat, troop, and support helicopters. Most utility and troop transport helicopters carried at least one or two door-mounted 7.62×51mm NATO M60D machine guns, to providing covering fire against enemy troops around "hot" landing zones. The most common helicopter types used by the Air Cav – the variants of the UH-1 "Huey" series – could go into action positively bristling with armament, including (on the Aerial Rocket Artillery (ARA) UH-1 "Huey Hog") two forward-firing M60Cs, two door-mounted M60Ds (one each side), and 2.75in (70mm) rocket pods either side. Airmobile firepower received a faster, more maneuverable platform from 1967 in the shape of the AH-1G HueyCobra, a dedicated helicopter gunship that could be armed with rocket pods, M129

The 1st Air Cav had organic artillery assets to provide on-call fire support. Here we see an Air Cav 105mm towed howitzer engaging enemy positions during Operation *Henry Clay*, a search-and-destroy mission conducted near the Cambodian border in July 1966. (NARA 100310266/ Wikimedia/Public Domain)

A member of 2d Pltn, Co. D, 2/7 Cav, 3d Bde, pauses on patrol near Ap My Thanh in March 1968, as part of Operation *Jeb Stuart*. On his back is an M72 Light Antitank Weapon (LAW), a 66mm portable one-shot unguided antitank rocket launcher that entered service in 1963. With an effective flat-trajectory range of 200m (219yd), the weapon was primarily designed for destroying enemy armor with its shaped-charge warheads, but it was also useful for engaging enemy bunkers and strongpoints with precision. (Staff Sergeant Harold C. Breedlove, DASPO, NARA 111-CCV-364-CC47352/ Wikimedia/Public Domain)

40mm grenade launchers, rotary 7.62mm M134 Miniguns, or a 20mm XM125 cannon. Such assets could unleash tremendous firepower in close support of infantry operations, and if rotary-wing assets were not sufficient, then fixed-wing strike-fighter attacks could be called in, depending on availability and mission viability, these aircraft unleashing heavy ordnance in the form of general-purpose, napalm, and white phosphorus bombs.

In terms of practical infantry-vs.-infantry fighting, the picture is slightly more nuanced. If we take out aerial and tube artillery from the equation (a not unreasonable decision – see 'Tactics' below), and given that terrain and airmobility often precluded the use of armor, the 1st Air Cav was armed in much the same way as any other US Army infantry division of the 1960s, albeit somewhat lighter than a regular ground infantry division to suit its airmobile role.

The 5.56×45mm NATO M16 assault rifle and the improved M16A1 (introduced in 1967) represented something of a revolution in American military small arms. Light, easy to handle (even on full-auto), and firing a high-velocity "intermediate" rifle round, the M16 was adopted into US Army use in 1963 as a replacement for the heavier 7.62×51mm NATO M14 battle rifle. There were some significant early reliability issues with the M16, however, related mainly to problems with ammunition (causing excessive carbon buildup in the chamber) and cleaning instructions, so the period 1965–67 saw much controversy concerning the weapon's adoption.

The belt-fed, bipod-mounted M60 machine gun was the standard squad support weapon, ripping through belts of ammunition at 550–650rd/min, and firing bullets weighty enough to slash through Vietnam's dense undergrowth. It had good shooting characteristics, with controllable recoil and a manageable rate of fire. Like the M16, however, it had more than its fair share of reliability and practicality issues. To name a few: it was prone to jamming in normal dirty field conditions (but worked well in the clear-air conditions of helicopter mounts); gas-mechanism components could work loose, resulting in a "runaway" gun, firing through the belt uncontrollably; it was heavy and unbalanced, making it awkward to carry for long periods; there was no adjustable gas regulator, meaning that the gunner could not adjust the gas pressure to compensate for a dirty weapon; and the quick-change barrel and bipod were an integral unit, making barrel changes awkward two-man affairs. It consequently acquired the nickname "The Pig."

Known as the "Blooper," on account of its hollow, gulping report, the 40mm M79 was a single-shot, break-barrel grenade launcher, firing a variety of antipersonnel and smoke rounds. Maximum range was 400m (437yd), and in skilled hands it could launch six rounds a minute. The M79 was a heavy item to carry (6.45lb loaded) in addition to a rifle, but it was accurate and undeniably useful for adding explosive power to the US infantry squad.

PAVN

It is impossible to be definitive concerning the weaponry within PAVN forces. Unlike the United States, with its unrivaled military-industrial facilities, North Vietnam had limited indigenous weapon-production capacity, and therefore it relied almost exclusively upon supplies from China, the Soviet Union, and Warsaw Pact countries, liberally supplemented with captured US/ARVN weaponry plus legacy firepower from the First Indochina War (1946–54) and even the war against the Japanese (1940–45). We cannot lay out, therefore, a neat TO&E when it comes to PAVN/VC weapons. We can, however, note some of the most important weapon types when it came to the clashes with the 1st Air Cav during the 1960s.

Because of the PAVN's limited logistical infrastructure when operating in South Vietnam (at least prior to the Tet Offensive), organic weaponry had to suit the requirements of portability and convenience. For regiments, the heaviest elements of firepower were contained in recoilless rifle, mortar, and antiaircraft companies. Recoilless rifles gave the PAVN a useful direct-fire "punch" against US armor and reinforced positions. Notable types in service were the 82mm Soviet B-10, 73mm SPG-9 *Kopye* (Spear), and captured US 57mm M18s and 75mm M20s (plus their Chinese copies: respectively, the Type 36 and Type 52/56). Although the recoilless rifles were at least notionally manportable, they were still hefty and awkward beasts to carry in mountainous and jungled terrain. Far more convenient were the 40mm RPG-2 and RPG-7 shoulder-launched rocket-propelled grenade launchers, supplied by the Soviet Union and (in copied forms) China; North Vietnam also locally produced versions of the RPG-2, known as the B40 and (with a larger bore) B50. The shrieking passage of a rocket-propelled grenade would be the signature sound of many of the US battles against the PAVN, a threat not only to troops and armor but also to US helicopters as they flew into "hot" LZs, where the enemy contested the landing as it was taking place.

For indirect fire, the PAVN operating in South Vietnam mainly relied upon a variety of mortars, although conventional Soviet/Chinese-supplied tube artillery became more common as the war went on. The key types of mortar in Vietnamese service were the Chinese Type 31 (a copy of the US 60mm M2), the Soviet 82mm 82-PM-37 (or the Chinese Type 37 copy) or 82-PM-41, and, at the heavier end of the scale, the 120mm 120-PM-43. Mortars were ideal tools for the jungle warfare that was so often fought in South Vietnam, for in the absence of artillery fire bases they provided the PAVN with significant localized firepower up to ranges of about 5,700m (6,234yd), in the case of the 120mm weapon.

The other main source of support fire was the PAVN's machine guns. In the infantry squads, light Soviet machine-gun types (and their inevitable Chinese copies) proliferated, particularly the 7.62×39mm RPD (Type 56 and North Korean Type 62) and RPK light machine guns, the 7.62×54mmR DP/DPM light machine guns (plus their Chinese Type 53 and 56 variants), and the 7.62×54mmR PK and SG-43/SGM medium machine guns that gave better penetration and range. Antiaircraft companies had up to 12 of the 12.7×108mm DShK heavy machine guns, thumping beasts with a maximum

In a rather jaunty propaganda image, a North Vietnamese soldier is helped from a tunnel complex. Note the narrow width of the entrance – many burlier US soldiers struggled to enter such tunnels. Note also that these soldiers are armed with captured or historic US weapons: the .30-caliber M1 Carbine (right) and the .30-06-caliber M1 Garand rifle. (Keystone-France/Gamma-Keystone via Getty Images)

The DShK heavy machine gun was the PAVN and VC's primary front-line antiaircraft weapon, as well as being used in ground-fire roles. This weapon is fitted with the dual antiaircraft sight, designed so that between them the gunner and loader could apply the correct amount of lead to the firing pattern. (Sovfoto/Universal Images Group via Getty Images)

range of 2,500m (2,734yd). These were burdensome weapons to haul around a jungle, however – the weight of the gun alone was 74.9lb, more than double that with a stable tripod mount – but they provided the PAVN forward units with a potent short-range antiaircraft capability; a couple of on-target bursts from one of these could easily bring down a UH-1 or larger airborne target.

At least until the PAVN opened its phase of open conventional war from 1968, which saw the use of more armor and tube artillery, the weapons listed above plus cognate types and the usual collection of demolitions and grenades represented the limits of PAVN front-line firepower. In essence, therefore, the PAVN was only equipped for short- to medium-range tactical infantry engagements. Extend the range out to any significant distance, and the PAVN forces were largely impotent, a reality that had a profound implication for PAVN tactics (see below).

The gap left by the absence of long-range weapons was to some degree filled by the PAVN's ever-growing skill with mines and booby traps. Distributed in large numbers around predicted enemy avenues of movement, they inflicted an infuriatingly consistent attrition on US troops, even without an accompanying infantry engagement. The preference of US troops was to move on trails, but when booby traps took too heavy a toll in a given area, they found it necessary to stay off the paths, which consequently slowed down the speed of advance and also cut the range that could be traveled in any given time period.

One final element of PAVN firepower deserves a mention: the 7.62×39mm AK-47 assault rifle, a revolutionary piece of Soviet engineering that became the PAVN's standard-issue personal weapon in the second half of the 1960s. It is hard to think of a more perfect firearm for the North Vietnamese soldiers than the AK-47, a selective-fire weapon firing from a 30-round box magazine at 600rd/min. Not particularly accurate, nor offering any significant advantages in power and range over the American weapons, the AK-47's crowning strength was its astonishing levels of reliability, a virtue much appreciated in the rust-inducing environment of the Vietnamese jungles. In combat, the AK-47 would rarely if ever fail its user – something that could not always be said for some of the American small arms.

The CH-54A Tarhe provided the 1st Air Cav with its most powerful heavy-lift tool. This particular helicopter has a large cargo pod fitted in the center, but the Tarhe's "skeletal" design meant that it could be adapted to lifting a great variety of underslung loads. (NARA 541861/ Wikimedia/Public Domain)

LOGISTICS AND MOBILITY

US Air Cav

For the Air Cav, the achievement of major tactical movements quickly across a theater formed their *raison d'être*. The Air Cav was fully airmobile. Large intra-theater lifts of men and equipment were provided by the big fixed-wing transporters – the two-engine CV-2A/B Caribou and C-123B/K Provider, and the four-engine C-130A/B/E Hercules – while tactical air mobility came from the fleet of helicopters. These could be divided into the heavy-lift types, such as the twin-rotor CH-47A and (from 1967) CH-47B Chinook and the single-rotor CH-54A Tarhe. The CH-47A had a maximum payload of about 10,000lb and could carry 33 troops internally, or a 105mm howitzer as an underslung load. The CH-54A had double the payload, at 20,000lb, meaning it could lift light tanks, individual UH-1 helicopters, heavy artillery pieces, and plentiful supplies. Yet the bulk of the in-theatre movement, particularly of troops, was done by the UH-1s, specifically the UH-1B/C/Ds during 1963–67, with the UH-1H entering service in late 1967. The UH-1D was the more capacious of the troop-lift variants, capable of carrying up to 11 troops at once; other versions were generally able to move about six troops at a time.

The vast resources of rotary-wing lift available to the Air Cav meant that they had almost total logistical and tactical freedom of movement across the AO, able to deliver supplies and troops rapidly across hundreds of kilometers of territory in a matter of minutes or mere hours. The 60 UH-1Ds of a single assault helicopter aviation battalion, for example, could move 660 men in one airlift. The constraints on this process were principally those of terrain – the helicopter pilots needed a viable LZ or drop zone to put their loads down – and weather. The latter could be particularly problematic during the monsoon seasons and also generally in the mountains, which were prone to low cloud ceilings and treacherous wind movements. The other constraint was, of course, enemy activity; PAVN and Viet Cong units would do their level best to prevent helicopters landing (see 'Tactics' below). There was also the problem of flight paths taking the helicopters through the arc of friendly artillery fire. It was not an uncommon experience for US helicopters and fixed-wing aircraft to be lost to shell strikes during campaigns. Still, despite

During Operation *Pershing*, a search-and-destroy operation that involved the 1st Air Cav for much of 1967, a mortar-platoon squad leader of 1/12 Cav stops to drink fresh coconut milk in the village of Troun Lan, Binh Dinh Province, approximately 90km (56 miles) northeast of An Khe. (NARA 530614/Wikimedia/Public Domain)

the constraints, it was evident that when it came to the both the tactical and strategic movement of logistics, US forces could set and establish a tempo that the enemy just could not match.

PAVN

In material terms, US forces in Vietnam eclipsed the PAVN in almost every regard (except simplicity and economy). This inequality was particularly expressed in terms of logistics and mobility, especially in the context of the PAVN-vs.-Air Cav battle.

PAVN logistical requirements seemed bewilderingly low to many US intelligence analysts. Logistics for a PAVN division operating in South Vietnam were placed at just 15 tons a day; a US division might consume at least six times that amount, and anything up to 500 tons depending on the nature of the operation. The reasons for the PAVN austerity can be traced mostly to the lean living characteristic of the society from which the soldiers were recruited. Daily life in the civilian world in North Vietnam was generally hard to begin with, so expectations regarding rations and equipment were similarly low in the armed services. A typical weight of *daily* rations for a PAVN soldier was just 2.7lb, usually in the form of dried rice – the *individual* meal carton of the US Meal, Combat, Individual (MCI) weighed about the same. We should not explain the contrast in rations entirely on account of PAVN dietary discipline, however. Much of a PAVN soldier's food would be supplied directly by the South Vietnamese people, either willingly or by forced requisition or "taxation." Indeed, one of the major objectives of US

search-and-destroy missions was to find the numerous PAVN/VC supply caches dotted around the South Vietnamese countryside. Prior to 1968, much of this South Vietnamese supply network was administered by the VC, but the PAVN took over more after the VC suffered severe casualties during the Tet Offensive.

The primary supply network feeding into South Vietnam was the "Ho Chi Minh Trail," as the Americans called it – to the North Vietnamese it was the Truong Son Strategic Supply Route. The Trail ultimately consisted of some 19,000km (12,000 miles) of paths, tracks, roads, improvised bridges, and waterways, punctuated by major logistical depots called *Binh Trams*, plus other smaller marshaling areas. The sinewy and organic nature of the Trail, plus the extraordinary resilience of the Group 559 transportation and logistical unit that kept it running, meant that even the relentless hammer blows of US heavy aerial bombing could never entirely cut the Trail.

Along the Ho Chi Minh Trail, and also the Sihanouk Trail in Cambodia, the PAVN pushed hundreds of tons of weapons, ammunition, food, and other equipment every day. The means by which they did so offer lessons in human ingenuity and stamina. Although trucks, jeeps, and other vehicular transport systems were used, their visibility to US reconnaissance aircraft, and the bomb-smashed nature of the jungle roads, meant that they could never be relied upon solely. Therefore, manpower and pack-animal power were the bedrock of PAVN logistics, especially once PAVN troops crossed into South Vietnam, where vehicle transport was virtually impossible. Bicycles were adapted to carry heavy loads on bamboo poles; two men might carry an 80lb load on a single pole between their shoulders, or 65–80lb on a back-mounted A-frame. A pack animal (mule or ox) could carry 130–200lb of supplies. The system was certainly successful: between 1965 and 1971 North Vietnam moved more than 630,000 troops, 400,000 weapons, 50,000 tons of ammunition, and 100,000 tons of food into South Vietnam along the Ho Chi Minh Trail.

The main resupply problem for the PAVN came during battle itself, particularly in relation to ammunition. While US air assets could generally keep new stocks of ammunition flowing into a combat zone, the PAVN had only limited capacity to replenish their stocks during the action, as they were limited by human carriage and local stocks. US soldiers would therefore often note a diminution of enemy firepower as the battle went on.

TACTICS

US Air Cav

An airmobile assault was a testing enterprise, involving rigorous planning and timetabling between multiple elements – aviation assets (assault, gunships, and logistics), supporting artillery, infantry units (including external US and ARVN forces), etc. – but with enough tactical flexibility to cope with the inevitable fog of war. Here we can provide a bare-bones outline (see Rottman 2007 for more in-depth coverage).

The planning that went into an airmobile assault focused upon strict timetabling and complex calculations. Once the mission objectives had been clarified, the planners had to crunch the numbers relating to lift requirements: numbers/types of aircraft; fuel and ammunition requirements; lift times and frequencies; routes and altitudes (multiple routes would be planned to a single LZ, to prevent the enemy finding predictable targets); weather conditions; coordination with artillery, and innumerable other considerations. Selection of the LZ was an especially crucial factor: it ideally had to be close to the

A repository of PAVN weapons captured by US forces in May 1968. The stash consists mainly of mortar bombs and shaped-charge missiles for rocket-propelled grenades. It was noted by the captors that many of the weapons displayed Russian or Chinese markings, indicating their source of origin. (Jonathan F. Abel Collection (COLL/3611), Marine Corps Archives & Special Collections, USMC/ Wikimedia/CC BY 2.0)

objective, but not right in the middle of the enemy (although sometimes that was necessary to achieve the element of surprise), nor so distant that the infantry would have an exhausting overland march to the objective. The physical LZ also had to be suitable to handle touchdown by helicopters, being ideally flat or of a viable gradient (no more than a 15-degree angle) and without adverse crosswinds. On occasions, teams of engineers might be inserted into an intended LZ to clear obstacles and troublesome vegetation, although this activity naturally alerted the enemy to a forthcoming action. Often, however, the nature of the terrain meant that troop-carrying helicopters would instead hover just above the ground to disgorge their occupants – a recipe for a considerable number of twisted ankles or knees.

In the case of many LZs, the surrounding area would often be "prepped" with 10-minute artillery bombardments, the barrage lifting when the assault aviation was two minutes out. (It is for this reason that "hot" LZs became relatively rare as the war progressed.) Artillery suppression was appreciated by troops going in to land, but the resulting devastation of the landscape could make movement through the terrain even more awkward. As the assault elements approached the LZ, "Pink Team" reconnaissance missions would be flown ahead by OH-6A light observation helicopters acting as surveillance platforms, supported by AH-1G helicopter gunships to deliver further suppressive fire on identified targets. The first troops to land in the LZ would act as a control party, establishing the status of the LZ, securing it for subsequent landings, and liaising with the Pink Teams and the airmobile

A staff sergeant of the 9th Cavalry shows the basic infantry gear of the mid-1960s in Vietnam. He has the M1956 webbing system with two ammunition pouches for his M16 assault rifle, plus two M18 smoke grenades to the front and one M26 fragmentation grenade on his side. (US Army Heritage and Education Center/Wikimedia/Public Domain)

force commander. Every subsequent lift would expand the combat power of the force, the heavy-lift helicopters bringing in more firepower, including mortars and tube artillery if required. The flight of UH-1s would land in "V" formations, and the soldiers would pile out at great speed, forming a perimeter for subsequent flights, if any, to come in. If soldiers were reinforcing a unit that was already locked in combat with an enemy force, they would be dropped off nearby, often in the secured LZ in the rear of the combat zone, which they would then use to process the wounded and dead and to receive supplies. Most operations were designed to land a force that would then move quite some distance in coordination with other units that had landed elsewhere, the object being to make contact with an enemy who was concealed and whose whereabouts were unknown.

Once the Air Cav soldiers moved away from the LZ, they would fight like conventional infantry. The search-and-destroy missions of the 1960s varied in duration from a few days to several months, during which time the US troops might make multiple assault lifts between objectives. The on-ground tactics were dictated by the mission. Typical objectives might be to "pacify" a contested area by destroying identified enemy units or bases, cutting supply routes, or searching villages and remote locations for arms or supply caches. The bedrock of US tactics was fire-and-maneuver: fire – putting down lots of lead and explosives to inflict attrition, fix enemy units in place, and to force their heads down, and maneuver – leapfrogging forward and encircling, trapping, or outflanking the enemy. Commonly, airmobile operations would involve landings at multiple widely separated LZs to create a "hammer-and-anvil" attack, with one unit acting as a blocking force (the anvil) against which the advancing unit (the hammer) would smash the enemy. Frequently, when the US troops met intensive resistance, they would retreat to a reasonably safe distance and call in major strikes, ranging from a single napalm pass from an A-1 Skyraider to area destruction by B-52 Stratofortress strategic bombers.

PAVN

The problem for the US soldiers, as we will see below, was that large-scale actions frequently devolved into grim small-unit scraps, fought at close quarters in restricted terrain that prohibited swift ground movement. In these instances, PAVN troops could more than hold their own, at least until the heavier US firepower could be brought to bear. Although 1965–67 was a period in which PAVN forces did make efforts to mount conventional ground offensives, culminating in the Tet Offensive launched in late January 1968, they still largely practiced the tactics of guerrilla warfare. These involved a heavy reliance upon ambushes, remote attrition via mines and booby traps, sabotage, and strikes against US bases. Speaking very generally, the US forces sought big battles and high enemy body counts – often the only metric of success the US forces applied to a campaign – while the PAVN avoided them, although sometimes they were unavoidable. PAVN units would move their positions and bases frequently, and could disperse and hide efficiently in the terrain, making them an elusive enemy. They became particularly adept at engaging US forces with a small, committed rearguard to give the impression

What appears to be either a PAVN column or a Main Force VC unit marches along what the original caption information claims to be the Ho Chi Minh Trail in September 1966. Such use of open roads was highly inadvisable at this stage of the war, and it is likely a staged propaganda photograph. (Sovfoto/Universal Images Group via Getty Images)

that the units were still in place, while the bulk of the soldiers disappeared through any gaps left in US attempts at encirclement (see the Analysis chapter for more consideration of this tactic). They also used preplanned re-concentration sites: their soldiers would all take different circuitous routes to this site, which scattered the unit all over the landscape so that it could not, as a whole, be intercepted or wiped out. This tactic was an ingenious way of sustaining a complete rout without the total destruction of the force.

In terms of countering airmobile operations, the PAVN's first line of defense could be to send up heavy fire against US helicopters as they approached a landing zone. This not only involved hails of standard small-arms fire, but also fire from heavier automatic weapons, such as tripod-mounted DShK heavy machine guns or even 20mm cannon. Troops might also prepare defenses within a predicted LZ: sowing mines, setting up machine-gun fields of fire, and stringing up obstructing cables. Around the LZ and AO, troops were also adept at preparing low-key but resilient defensive positions, using sandbags, logs, and foliage to create strongpoints in much the same way the Japanese did during World War II.

Also as the Japanese learned, and following Soviet doctrine, the PAVN developed tactics to limit the dominance of US firepower in infantry-vs.-infantry combat. By "hugging" the US units – staying close to them and fighting at close quarters (also called "grab and hold") – PAVN forces could prevent US troops calling in air strikes or artillery support. Any bombardments closer than 600m (656yd) are classified as "danger close" for friendly forces, meaning that they are threatened by their own fire. Understanding this, PAVN forces would typically try to stay within 100–200m (109–219yd) of their opponents during a firefight. Such ranges, and frequently less, were often compelled anyway by the nature of the terrain, as visibility was frequently limited by surrounding foliage.

Operation *Masher*

January 28–February 3, 1966

BACKGROUND TO BATTLE

In 1965–66, the PAVN made increasingly sizable infiltrations into South Vietnam, where the North Vietnamese forces established mobile bases and logistics hubs and launched attacks against US and ARVN units. The 1st Air Cav had already been bloodied in the battle against this buildup, first during the lifting of the siege of Plei Me (a US Special Forces camp in the Central Highlands) during October 19–25, 1965. This action contributed to the later epic four-day clash between the Air Cav and two PAVN regiments during the battle of Ia Drang (November 14–18, 1965), an engagement that has gone down as a sobering milestone in Air Cav history, with US forces taking 499 casualties, although PAVN losses were at least three times greater. This battle provided the Air Cav with a brutal object lesson in how to fight the PAVN, knowledge that would be applied in the clashes of 1966.

Operation *Masher* was to be a major multibattalion search-and-destroy operation conducted in late January and February 1966 in the heavily populated Binh Dinh Province on the northeastern coastline of South Vietnam, in II CTZ. By 1966, US intelligence had become aware of a PAVN buildup in the province: the 6,000-strong 3d PAVN Division, composed of two regiments of regular PAVN troops and one regiment of Main Force VC. There was the fear that if this infiltration went unchecked, the province might simply pass irrevocably into communist control.

The overall objective of Operation *Masher* – which the 1st Air Cav, plus the 22d ARVN Infantry Division and the Republic of Korea Army's Capital Division, were charged to fulfill – was to clear the Bong Son Plain in the north of the province and adjacent valleys and mountains, particularly the An Lao

and Kim Son river valleys and the Cay Giep mountains. The action would be a classic airmobile action, and would be the conflict's largest search-and-destroy operation to date.

Some clarification of terminology is required before proceeding. Operation *Masher* is also referred to as Operation *Masher/White Wing*, on account of the fact that President Lyndon B. Johnson later changed the name of *Masher* to *White Wing*, feeling that the new name would send less-belligerent signals to the US public than the merciless *Masher*. Strictly speaking, Operation *Masher* (the clearance of the Bong Son Plain) ran from January 25 through February 6, 1966, while Operation *White Wing* took over from February 6 through March 5. There were further operational subdivisions of the *White Wing* phase. A US Pacific Air Forces (PACAF) report from September 1966 breaks down the campaign and its objectives into four phases and objectives:

> Operation *Masher*: January 24–February 6 (the dates include the initial deployment phases) – search-and-destroy mission in the Bong Son Plain.
> Operation *White Wing*: February 6–15 – battalion sweeps through the An Lao Valley.
> Operation *Eagle Claw*: February 11–27 – a continuation of *White Wing* in the An Lao Valley.
> Operation *Black Horse*: March 1–5 – a search-and-destroy mission into the Cay Giep mountains southeast of Bong Son. (HQ PACAF 1965)

Note, however, that there is some official variation in the date parameters of the different operations. A 1st Air Cav after-action report, for example, has *Masher* ending on February 3, with *White Wing* beginning on February 4.

Here we will look in detail at the Operation *Masher* action, conducted by 3d Bde, 1st Air Cav. The specific PAVN units which would challenge the Americans are not known with absolute clarity, particularly at the battalion level. We do know, however, that the principal units encountered on the Bong Son Plain were the 7th and 9th battalions of the 22d (Quyet Tam) Regiment.

Operation *Masher* can be viewed in the overall context of General Westmoreland's "search-and-destroy" strategy. Westmoreland had to arrive at some sort of metric to indicate US progress toward "victory," which was vaguely conceived as the pacification of communist forces in South Vietnam, to the extent that North Vietnam was no longer able to prosecute the war. Although search-and-destroy could be intellectually packaged in various different ways, it was overwhelmingly an attrition-based tactic – what mattered was that US forces found the enemy combatants, deployed in force, and killed as many of them as possible. Operation *Masher* would also result in a significant number of North Vietnamese prisoners for US forces, although sometimes it was hard to distinguish enemy personnel from civilians. The men squatting here are all VC suspects. Note the rice-paddy furrows, which often provided emergency cover during firefights. (Bettmann via Getty Images)

MAP KEY

1 **January 24–25:** 2/7 Cav and 2/12 Cav are airlifted by C-123K transport aircraft to the Bong Son area from An Khe, in readiness for operations farther north. During the movement on the 25th, one of the aircraft carrying a platoon from Co. A, 2/7 Cav crashes into a mountain in the An Khe Pass, killing 42 infantry and four aircrew.

2 **January 25:** 1/7 Cav is airlifted to LZ George in the southeast of the area of operations. The battalion strikes out to the northeast, making a diversionary advance to secure elevated terrain southeast of Bong Son, and encounters moderate resistance on the way.

3 **0800hrs, January 26:** 2/7 Cav is air assaulted north to LZ Dog. There are some intense infantry engagements here requiring the heavy use of US air power to suppress the resistance.

4 **January 28:** 1/7 Cav moves up to LZ Papa. Meanwhile, 2/7 Cav moves up to LZ 4, encountering a hard PAVN defense and losing four CH-47As on the approach.

5 **January 29:** 2/12 Cav moves up to the right flank of 1/7 Cav, which is still fighting for survival around LZ 4.

6 **January 30–31:** 2/12 Cav slowly begins to push north out of the LZ area. Meanwhile, 1/7 Cav is engaged around LZ Romeo on January 31. 1/5 Cav (-) joins the efforts in the north of the area of operations.

7 **February 1–2:** 1/7 Cav starts sweeping west toward LZ Quebec, then moves up to secure Position Steel. 2/12 Cav also turns west to establish blocking positions, while 1/9 Cav arrives to support efforts southwest of Position Steel.

8 **February 3:** By the end of the operation, the PAVN units, identified as three battalions of the 22d (Quyet Tam) Regiment, have dispersed throughout the AO, being unable to hold their positions against the US advances and the overwhelming firepower.

Battlefield environment

The Bong Son Plain is a relatively narrow coastal strip, about 25km (15.5 miles) across at its widest points. It is bisected on an east–west axis by the Lai Giang River, which runs just below the township of Bong Son itself, and by Highway 1 on a north–south axis. For Operation *Masher*, the plain presented a mix of terrains – sandy beachfront, palm groves and coastal forests, rough scrubland, sections of coastal jungle, agricultural terraces reaching up to 295ft in height, elevated spurs running off the mountains, and steep-sided river valleys. The climate would also provide an obstacle to airmobile operations; the weather during Operation *Masher* would be unpredictable, with hours of sunshine followed by heavy rain, fog, or low cloud, sometimes intense enough to place restrictions upon both fixed- and rotary-wing air operations.

A soldier of the 1st Air Cav squats down to inspect an enemy underground bunker during Operation *Masher*. On arrival in a village, a PAVN unit might take no more than two hours to construct its defensive positions, including bunkers, trenches, and firing positions. (© CORBIS/Corbis via Getty Images)

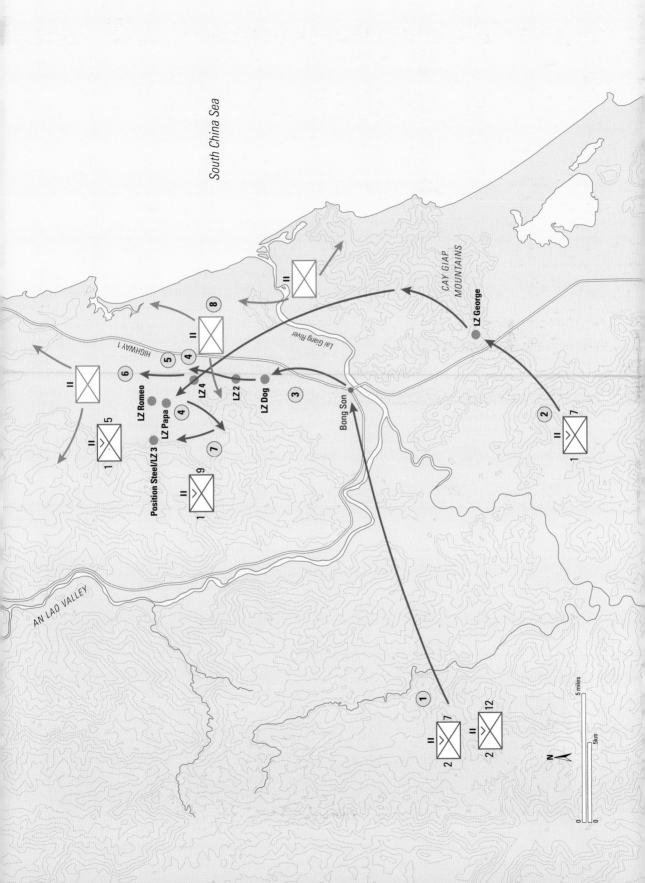

South China Sea

CAY GIAP MOUNTAINS

LZ George

Lai Giang River

HIGHWAY 1

LZ Romeo

LZ Papa

Position Steel/LZ 3

LZ 4

LZ 2

LZ Dog

Bong Son

AN LAO VALLEY

5 miles

5km

N

8

5

4

6

4

7

3

2

1

9 1

5 1

7 1

7 2

12 2

INTO COMBAT

Operation *Masher* began with the movement, on January 24, of the 3d Bde from its base at An Khe to a forward base at Phu Cat, to the southeast of Bong Son; this movement, classified as Phase I of the operation, was a big lift of four battalions, by road transportation and also by US Air Force C-123K transport aircraft plus the Air Cav's own UH-1Ds and CH-47A helicopters (Phu Cat included an air base). The advance out of Phu Cat, or the beginning of Operation *Masher* proper, was initiated on January 25, and consisted of two independent thrusts: 1/7 Cav struck out toward the southern reaches of the Chop Chai hill, just to the southeast of Bong Son, deploying the battalion to LZ George (this was to act as a diversionary attack, and also to provide security across the important Highway 1), while 2/7 Cav struck north through Bong Son to LZ Dog. Its objective was to clear the land north of Bong Son and establish a forward command post and support outpost.

The morning of the 25th, therefore, was split by the harsh sound of hundreds of rotating rotor blades and the roar of aero engines, as the cavalry units moved forward en masse, the Air Cav's helicopters flying low and fast across to their LZ objectives. During the landing at LZ Dog, US Air Force air support, in the form of A-1E ground-attack strikes, hit the limited numbers of North Vietnamese defenders just west of the LZ hard with napalm, white phosphorus, high-explosive, and 20mm ordnance. In terms of enemy contact, the first day of Operation *Masher* provided little in the way of serious threat. Both battalions triggered only light resistance – the occasional burst of small-arms fire or the crump of a mortar round – and they managed to push forward to their objectives with little impediment. The biggest tragedy resulted from an accident, rather than combat: Co. A, 2/7 Cav – a veteran company that

Troops of the 1st Cavalry Division's Reconnaissance Unit move quickly to take up a defensive position in the middle of a rice paddy near Bong Son. The platoon took enemy fire immediately upon landing, as they began a scouting operation in the area to support the brigade action. (Bettmann via Getty Images)

had suffered heavily at the battle of Ia Drang – lost its entire 3d Pltn and a mortar squad when a C-123K flying out of An Khe plunged into the side of a mountain in the An Khe Pass shortly after takeoff. There were no survivors; 42 Air Cav men were killed, plus the four-man aircrew. It was a horrific start to the operation, yet there was no choice but to carry on.

Action started to intensify somewhat on the 26th. Just to the northeast of LZ Dog, Cos B and C, 2/7 Cav came into contact with small numbers of PAVN regulars, receiving small-arms fire in the process. The infantry halted and again the A-1Es were called in, pummeling the identified locations. Interestingly, the US troops found no bodies when the resumed their movement forward, but there were indications of egress out of the area.

The movements and intentions of the PAVN during this time are largely unknown. Certainly, by mid-morning on the 25th they would have been aware that a major US operation was being launched in Binh Dinh Province. Initial contacts were very light, suggesting that either the US troops were advancing into areas with limited PAVN presence or, more likely, that the North Vietnamese forces were readjusting their positions accordingly. During the fight to the northeast of LZ Dog, US soldiers reported seeing khaki uniforms, meaning that regular PAVN troops were certainly in the area. Meanwhile, the civilian population was suffering under heavy US aerial and artillery bombardments; between January 25 and 28, US artillery units delivered more than 2,000 rounds onto targets around the area of operations. A total of 45 US Air Force ground-attack sorties were also delivered between the 25th and 27th, in response to immediate requests for air cover.

The tempo of combat changed significantly on the 28th. This was the beginning of Phase II of Operation *Masher*:

> … with airmobile and ground attacks north up the coastal plain by the 2/7 Cav, air landing of the 1/7 Cav on the high ground to the west, then attacking to the east. The 2/12 Cav was to be landed in the northern end of the area of operation

ABOVE LEFT
A flight of UH-1s approach an LZ to deposit their troops. To keep exposure to enemy fire to an absolute minimum, each helicopter would typically hover for no more than six seconds to deposit its troops. (Underwood Archives/ Getty Images)

ABOVE RIGHT
When US soldiers deployed from a CH-47A helicopter – which because of its size could struggle to find suitable places to touch down – rope ladders might be used to climb down from the rear of the cargo hold. The two men at the bottom steady the rope ladder against the intense downwash of the rotor blades. (Bettmann via Getty Images)

and would attack to the south. Thus, with the ARVN on the east [the 22d ARVN Division was performing a security action along Highway 1], the enemy would be hit from four directions. (HQ PACAF 1966: 3)

As the report noted, however, poor weather would effect a change in the operation, although it was not only the weather that would challenge the US troops that day.

To the north of LZ Dog, and at the end of what was referred to as Position Steel, 2/7 Cav made its airmobile assault forward to LZs 3 and 4. The primary objectives were the hamlets called Cu Nghi and Phung Du. It was to be the beginning of a harrowing action. Illustrating the dangers to air assets from friendly artillery, three CH-47As were hit en route by artillery shells. Furthermore, while the landings at LZ 3 went largely uncontested, those at LZ 4 were met with dense automatic weapons fire from the trees and hedgerows that surrounded the hamlets. Here the North Vietnamese forces would evidently make a more determined stand. During the initial landing phase on the 28th, within an hour of taking off, four CH-47As were shot down and 12 UH-1Ds were significantly damaged. By 1500hrs that day, some 28 helicopters had taken serious hits.

The exact PAVN units fighting around LZ 4 are not clear; communist troops also likely included substantial VC elements. What was evident was that they were fighting from well-prepared defensive positions, including heavy machine guns emplaced in bunkers and trenches around the treelines, pre-sited to direct accurate fire upon approaching helicopters. Ironically, LZ 4 had been spared any sort of preparatory artillery bombardment or air strikes; the presence of many local villagers, and that of a revered cemetery at the southern end of Phung Du, meant that this time the communist forces were intact and waiting.

The first company of 2/7 Cav to go into the Phung Du was Co. C, led by Captain John A. "Skip" Fesmire. Taking heavy fire during the approach and immediately on touchdown, including mortar rounds, the company found itself scattered through the village, stretched out over several hundred yards and taking cover wherever they could find it, including behind the burial mounds in the cemetery. The fighting was at extreme close quarters, measured in tens of feet, and the Americans were by now taking serious casualties. In one instance, three men were hit by fire before they had even managed to step out of the helicopter. The Americans were also struggling to build up fire superiority. One soldier, Staff Sergeant William H. Guyer of the mortar platoon, had a 60mm mortar but no baseplate. He had to use the mortar by propping it up against a bank of earth. Despite the crude setup, he managed to drop a round onto the PAVN machine-gun team that was targeting the US troops. In the terrible, random reversals for which war is known, Guyer was then killed by fire from the same machine gun, fired by another PAVN soldier. That man was killed moments later by a mortar round fired by Sergeant Jose A. Rivera-Reyes, who was in turn then killed by a PAVN mortar bomb (McManus 2010). This was just one of the corners of tragedy on the battlefield around LZ 4.

There were some surreal moments of civilian interaction. During the afternoon, Co. B went into Phung Du as reinforcements, but all

LZ Dog, Operation *Masher*, January 28, 1966

US view: An Air Cav door gunner of Co. B, 2/7 Cav opens up on enemy machine-gunners as he is airlifted into LZ Dog around the hamlet of Phung Du during Operation *Masher*. This helicopter is part of the attempted relief force flown in to attempt the rescue of Co. C, which has been trapped in a desperate firefight with heavy PAVN and VC forces since the early hours of the morning. The machine-gunner is targeting muzzle flashes from enemy weapons in the treeline, firing with his 7.62×51mm M60D door-mounted machine gun, which was essentially the base-model M60 but fitted with spade grips. He is wearing the typical flight kit of the time, with the informality that comes with operational reality. He has Nomex flight trousers and a US Army sateen shirt, over the top of which is a basic body armor jacket. His helmet is the APH-5A (Army Protective Helmet No. 5); later in the 1960s, a ballistic version, the AFH-1 (Antifragmentation Flight Helmet No. 1), was introduced.

PAVN view: A two-man PAVN machine-gun team, manning a 12.7×108mm DShKM (M for Modernized) heavy machine gun, with a third infantryman in support, open fire on US helicopters as they come into the landing zone. The DShKM could bring down a UH-1 or heavier helicopter with relative ease, especially if it scored hits on the engine compartment, the main-rotor hub, or the tail rotor. Like most heavy machine guns it produced a fairly prodigious muzzle flash, one that US attack helicopters and their door gunners could zero in on fairly quickly. The three men are dressed in the characteristically plain uniforms of the PAVN, with belted olive-green base uniforms, green canvas and rubber boots, the North Vietnamese forces' pith helmet, and water canteens. The machine-gun team are accompanied by a third soldier who is armed with a 7.62×39mm Type 56 assault rifle, a Chinese copy of the AK-47. He is performing a tactical magazine change, replacing a partially empty magazine with a full one in preparation for the close action to come.

This PAVN antiaircraft team was actually photographed in North Vietnam, but was typical of the defensive threats US helicopters might face. The weapon is particularly interesting – a World War II-era German 7.92×57mm MG 34 general-purpose machine gun, fitted with a basic antiaircraft sight and a 75-round drum magazine. (Sovfoto/Universal Images Group via Getty Images)

the helicopters flew into storms of ground fire. At one point, an enemy machine-gunner, his weapon on an antiaircraft mount, was standing in the middle of a street, firing upward and surrounded by a crowd of seemingly impassive villagers. (They were doubtless present under duress.) One helicopter pilot ordered his door gunner to fire warning shots to scatter the villagers; amazingly, they stayed on the spot, so the door gunner was forced to fire directly into them to take out the machine-gunner. All six of the Co. B helicopters were hit by ground fire, and only a platoon of troops was actually deposited into LZ 4 (McManus 2010).

By the time night fell, and as the firefights continued in the darkness, it was clear to Lieutenant Colonel Harold G. "Hal" Moore, commander of the 3d Bde, that reinforcements would be needed to break the deadlock. The remainder of Co. A, 2/7 Cav (since the C-123K crash, now only two rifle platoons) was by this time moving north from around LZ 2 toward LZ 4, although an enemy blocking position retarded its progress significantly. Moore also ordered two companies of 2/12 Cav to air assault south of LZ 4, and move north to outflank the PAVN units. Meanwhile, 1/7 Cav was landed at LZ Papa, just to the west of Cu Nghi. The 9th Bn, 22d PAVN Regt, was waiting for them, putting the US troops under streams of machine-gun fire both during the approach to the LZ and again when they spread out around landing. The PAVN soldiers had an early result around LZ Papa, when they shot down a CH-47A, which was carrying an underslung 105mm howitzer. Obtaining a high-quality piece of tube artillery would be a minor victory for the PAVN, so they surged forward and engaged Co. B, 1/7 Cav – now the howitzer's defenders – in an intense firefight. The Co. B soldiers gave as good

Two Air Cav soldiers drag away a wounded PAVN soldier during Operation *Masher*. The ammunition belt around the soldier's waist likely contained clips for a 7.62×39mm SKS rifle, another of the other common types used by the PAVN alongside the AK-47 assault rifle. (Bettmann via Getty Images)

as they got, and eventually drove back the PAVN troops back by bringing the howitzer into action, utilizing it as a direct-fire weapon and blasting the attackers over open sights.

During January 29–30, it was clear that US firepower and the overwhelming mobile force were beginning to have an effect on the enemy. There were more signs that the PAVN was retreating, and the cavalry units deployed began to engage in pursuit operations. An official 1st Air Cav after-action report explains the complex details of the next three days:

29 Jan 66. Early on the morning of 29 Jan, the two companies of 2/7 Cav [A and C] linked up in LZ 4, but were still under intense enemy fire. The 2/12 air assaulted south of LZ 4 to maneuver north and flank the enemy. 1/7 Cav elements secured ROMEO north LZ 4. TAC Air worked over LZ 4 with napalm to assist the 2/7 Cav, getting many secondary explosions in the trenches. Enemy disposition included well fortified positions, deep trenches, and extensive tunneling. 2/12 Cav maneuvered towards LZ 4 to relieve the enemy pressure, and element of the 1/7 Cav north of LZ 4 met up blocking positions facing south to engage the fleeing enemy.

30 Jan 66. LZ 4 was still under heavy fire early on 30 Jan. Resistance decreased at dawn and extensive clearing operations began by 2/7 Cav while 2/12 Cav began moving slowly north of the LZ area into LZ MIKE and LZ TOM. Elements of 1/5 Cav were sent from the Division base area to Phu Cat to replace the 1/12. The 2/7 Cav confined their search and destroy missions to LZ 4 area.

1 Feb 66. 1/7 Cav started sweeping west toward psn QUEBEC. 2/12 Cav continued sweeping north and linked up with the 3rd APC Company of the

ARVN Division. 1/12 Cav established a blocking position at BS 865134 and 2/12 Cav turned west driving into the 1/12 blocking position. 1/7 Cav returned to vicinity LZ 4 while elements of the 2/7 Cav were securing the artillery at LZ MIKE and position DOG. Sporadic enemy resistance was encountered during the day. (HQ 1st Cavalry Division 1966: 14)

Some aspects of this report are worth exploring. First, the reference to the "well fortified positions, deep trenches, and extensive tunneling" illustrates just how established the PAVN was in the area, having had both the time and tactical space to construct such defenses, but also the expectation that they might be occupied for useful periods of time. In several locations, US soldiers had to explore underground in "tunnel rat" fashion, flashlight in one hand, and a hand gun in the other, in a definite test of nerve.

Second, the report acknowledges the constant support provided by air cover, which intensified as flying conditions improved. During 1/7 Cav's move toward LZ Romeo, for example, the battalion came under sniper fire from a village to the east; a napalm strike annulled the threat. As night approached on January 30, the same battalion also had to call a halt to a river crossing, as it took incoming fire. Four A-1E sorties hit the PAVN positions before dark, but the fighting continued through the night, the US Air Force providing overhead flareship illumination to hold back the darkness. According to the US soldiers, the PAVN soldiers would intensify their fire every time a dud flare failed to ignite. At 0515hrs the next morning, the battalion came under a direct assault from two companies of PAVN troops, but two A-1Es, directed by an Air Cav forward air controller

Although not taken during Operation *Masher*, this photograph gives a good impression of a PAVN small-unit offensive maneuver, the soldiers sprinting forward with AK-47 and SKS rifles. An offensive action like this would generally be performed against fixed enemy positions or when sensing an immediate tactical opportunity. Generally, however, the PAVN followed defensive tactics in 1966 and 1967, prior to the all-out Tet Offensive in January 1968. (Keystone/Getty Images)

(FAC), skidded napalm into the enemy-occupied treeline, with 90 percent target coverage. By 0900hrs, the two companies were withdrawing to the southwest and 1/7 Cav moved out in pursuit.

The overall picture given by the report is that of the US forces beginning to gain the maneuver advantage over the enemy, who was now dispersing and retreating, leaving behind an increasing number of dead on the battlefield. The PAVN troops scattered in small bands and broke out to the north, northwest, and west. It was not a complete rout, far from it. The PAVN fought some highly competent delaying actions, frequently pinning down US soldiers for long periods of time. Yet as the PAVN relinquished their "hug" on the US soldiers, they in turn became prey to the depredations of US air power and artillery, which became increasingly dangerous as they freed themselves from the restrictions of danger-close conditions. On February 2–3, for example, the US Air Force even began hitting enemy locations with B-52 aerial bombing strikes.

Operation *Masher* proper ended on February 6, with the PAVN forces largely neutralized, for now, on the Bong Son Plain, although that would not stop them moving back in later. Operation *White Wing* and its subsidiary operations, however, would continue until March 6, in the adjacent mountains and valleys. The actions fought in these continuation campaigns would, at times, be every bit as violent and contested as those of Operation *Masher*, and the Air Cav had to fight hard for every scrap of the terrain they captured. Regarding the body count, a report listed 603 enemy confirmed dead, another 956 estimated dead, 357 wounded (estimated), and 242 captured during Operation *Masher*. By the end of Operation *Masher/White Wing*, altogether the US collected figures were 1,342 killed (body count), an additional estimated 1,746 killed, 1,348 wounded, and 633 captured. These losses were undoubtedly a major blow to the PAVN, which lost about half the strength of the 3d Division. In the other column on the casualty board, US forces had also suffered heavily, despite their overwhelming advantages in mobility and firepower. Total US losses were 228 killed and 788 wounded. It was clear that whatever advantages the Air Cav had over the PAVN on paper, the fighting on the ground was almost never going to be purely one-sided.

What Operation *Masher/White Wing* had demonstrated, however, was the formidable capacity of US airmobility. The aforementioned HQ PACAF report noted that

Airlift, both Army and USAF, played a heavy role during the operation. Between 25 January and 6 March 1966, 9700.9 tons of cargo were airlifted along with 93,351 passengers. In all 78 infantry battalions and 55 artillery batteries were moved by air. The division kept at least four infantry battalions (and six for the majority of the period) in sustained operations for 41 days at an average distance from the An Khe base of 65 kilometers. (HQ PACAF 1966: 26)

Operation *Masher/White Wing* was a confident demonstration of the airmobile principle at work. What would remain a challenge would be how to fight the PAVN on the ground.

OPPOSITE
A US soldier steps around the bodies of enemy fighters killed around Phu Cat, 1966. Based on the scorched appearance of the ground around them, these enemy troops were likely killed by either an air strike or artillery bombardment. The American is collecting their weapons, including the AK-47 assault rifle he is holding. (Bettmann via Getty Images)

Operation *Crazy Horse*

May 16–June 5, 1966

BACKGROUND TO BATTLE

Operation *Crazy Horse* stands as an interesting counterpoint to the other operations covered in this book. Rather than being a preplanned action, *Crazy Horse* was rather an action that emerged out of developing circumstances. As such, it illustrates how the 1st Air Cav was able to use its airmobile talents in a rapid-reaction operation. On the PAVN side, Operation *Crazy Horse* shows

This photograph perfectly captures the physical challenge presented by jungle terrain for US operations. In these conditions, close-range ambushes were an ever-present threat, and it was easy for the PAVN and VC to conceal tripwires, mines, and other booby traps. (Bill Hall/ Michael Ochs Archives/ Getty Images)

a tactical rhythm that became common throughout the 1960s: PAVN forces would initially gain the localized initiative through ambush and intensive close-quarters fighting, but then steadily weaken in the face of US fire-and-maneuver tactics, before breaking the contact and attempting to flee the AO, usually leaving large numbers of their dead and wounded behind.

The context for the battle lay in the Vinh Thanh Valley, in Binh Dinh Province. Since they had deployed in September 1965 to Camp Radcliff at An Khe, just 16km (10 miles) northwest of the Vinh Thanh Valley, the 1st Air Cav had been engaged in reconnaissance and sweep operations through the region, which was known to be a basing area for VC and PAVN units. Operations in 1965 and the first few months of 1966 brought little contact with the enemy in the valley region, but that situation would change in May 1966.

On May 10, Special Forces soldiers from the Civilian Irregular Defense Group (CIDG) camp in the Vinh Thanh Valley captured a VC Local Force soldier, which led to a CIDG ambush on a VC platoon. Among the materials captured were instruments and calculations relating to the use of 120mm mortars and artillery, plus documents that suggested an attack on the CIDG camp was scheduled for May 19. In response, US Special Forces operatives contacted the 1st Air Cav HQ at An Khe, and asked for preemptive assistance. The commander of the division at that time, Major General John Norton, ordered the commander of the 1st Bde of the Air Cav, Colonel John Hennessey, to deploy elements of his brigade on a sweep through the region. This action led to a localized battle of such intensity that Norton was

A soldier of 5/7 Cav in action during a firefight, laying down rounds from his M16A1 assault rifle. At this point in time, the M16 used magazines that held just 20 rounds, which was inadequate to meet the needs of a heavy firefight. The basic infantry load was nine such magazines, for a total of 180 rounds, but experienced troops would carry much more. (US Army/Wikimedia/ Public Domain)

US troops fan out into the surrounding countryside after landing at LZ Hereford during Operation *Crazy Horse*. Note the 105mm M101A1 howitzers that have been emplaced in the LZ area, ready to deliver support fire into the surrounding mountains. (US Army Heritage and Education Center/ Wikimedia/Public Domain)

compelled to initiate a wider multibattalion operation – *Crazy Horse* – to engage the sizable PAVN forces which quite obviously were in the area.

The mission parameters for Operation *Crazy Horse*, when they were issued, were as follows (here presented in an after-action report):

9. MISSION. The division mission for Operation CRAZY HORSE, with the concurrence of I FFORCEV [Field Force Vietnam], was stated in 1st Cavalry Division (Airmobile) OPORD 6617 as "Division continues the attack to destroy enemy forces in the vicinity of the Vinh Thanh Valley (BR 6160); conducts offensive operations in vicinity of Division TAOR; conducts tactical route security on Highway 19 from BR 625471 to Pleiku City; and maintains a battalion TF reaction force for I FFORCEV and division."

10. CONCEPT OF OPERATION: a. The concept of operation in the 1st Cavalry Division OPORD 6617 was: "Division continues the attack against the 2d VC Regiment northeast of the Vinh Thanh Valley with 1st Brigade. Operations will be conducted so as to construct landing zones as quickly as possible, radically north and east of the present enemy contact along major routes and trails. Forces will be deployed into these landing zones to press the enemy against the forces now in contact. The enemy will be pursued regardless of his direction of movement. 2d Brigade maintains the I FFORCEV and division reserve/reaction force at Pleiku and conducts tactical route security on Highway 19 from An Khe to Pleiku. 3d Brigade secures the division base and conducts offensive operations in the TAOR."

b. The 1st Brigade was further directed to, "(1) Continue the attack in zone to destroy the 2d VC Regiment: Pursue the enemy regardless of his direction of movement. (2) Maximum effort will be made to capture a prisoner for intelligence purposes." (HQ 1st Cavalry Division 1966: 6)

Air Cav soldiers embark aboard CH-47A Chinook helicopters during Operation *Crazy Horse*. The Chinook was a challenging helicopter to fly in Vietnam, it being especially difficult to handle in the "hot-and-high" conditions frequently encountered in the Air Cav's areas of operations. (US Army/Wikimedia/Public Domain)

From the PAVN forces' perspective, their operational focus went from planning an aggressive localized attack on a Special Forces camp, to countering a powerful airmobile sweep that sought to shake them from their Vinh Thanh strongholds. The US intelligence was quite right – the principal unit in the area was the 2d VC Regt, a Main Force unit that came under the authority of the 3d PAVN Division. Other units confirmed as being in the area were the 14th Co., 32d Artillery Battalion (a 120mm mortar unit) and various Local Force and guerrilla VC companies, but as the fighting went on it further transpired that regular PAVN battalions were being fed into the battle, particularly the 8th (-) and 9th (-) battalions of the 22d PAVN Regt and the 6th Bn, 12th PAVN Regt. With such forces present in the valley, it was clear that the Air Cav was in for a fight.

In the account that follows, it should be noted that the movements of the Air Cav during Operation *Crazy Horse* were extremely complex, with multiple shifts of companies and battalions almost every day. Here our focus is purely on illustrating some of the main thrusts in the campaign. Note that the US units conducted near-constant sweeps of surrounding areas or remained in blocking positions.

MAP KEY

1 1100–2245hrs, May 16: Co. B, 2/8 Cav assaults into LZ Hereford and comes under extremely heavy enemy contact. It later receives reinforcement from Cos A and C, 1/12 Cav. The US forces establish a perimeter by nightfall.

2 0715–2400hrs, May 17: More reinforcements (1/5 Cav) are flown into LZ Hereford as the fighting escalates. US forces push out to the east against steady PAVN/VC resistance.

3 1047hrs, May 17: 2/12 Cav, having air assaulted into LZ Horse at 0640hrs, come under fire from PAVN/VC mortars. Despite tactical air support, the battalion is unable to advance before nightfall.

4 May 19: 1/12 Cav moves to secure the area around LZ Milton and LZ Hereford. Meanwhile, elements of 1/5 Cav conduct operations around LZ Monkey.

5 0848hrs, May 20: 1/5 Cav moves forward to LZ Ape, and consolidates the position.

6 1420hrs, May 20: 1/5 Cav assaults LZ Mortimer. Although there is little contact at first, PAVN/VC units begin probing attacks by nightfall.

7 1547hrs, May 21: Co. B, 1/8 Cav engages in a very heavy firefight with PAVN units just to the northeast of LZ Horse. Around this period, many of the Air Cav units are engaged in sweeps of their local areas to clear out PAVN/VC forces.

8 0650hrs, May 23: Two companies of 1/5 Cav make an overland advance from LZ Coral to LZ Harvard in the north of the area of operations.

9 0845hrs, May 23: Cos A and C, 1/8 Cav move to LZ Steer and conduct patrols in the area, largely without contact.

10 1718hrs, May 23: 2/8 Cav (-) moves to LZ Clemson and begins patrolling the area.

11 1830hrs, May 31: Co. A, 1/8 Cav, having made a northerly sweep, is moved to LZ Coral.

12 1330hrs, June 4: As Operation *Crazy Horse* comes to an end, Cos B and C, 1/8 Cav close down LZ Savoy and are extracted.

Battlefield environment

The terrain in the Vinh Thahn Valley, the bordering mountains, and, 16km (10 miles) east of Vinh Thanh Valley, the Suoi Ca Valley, was highly challenging for military operations, including airmobile actions. The 1st Air Cav after-action report provides an insight into the profound fluctuations of terrain: "The CRAZY HORSE AO covers approximately 1600 square kilometers. From a minimum altitude of 200 feet in the Vinh Thanh Valley, the altitude increases rapidly to 3000 feet in the center peaks. Dense vegetation with a high canopy with second and third growths underneath cover the mountains. Ground mobility is extremely difficult in the mountains except along the numerous intermittent streams running east into the Suoi Ca Valley and west into the Vinh Thanh Valley. In the center of the AO, the mountains rise sharply from the stream beds and sheer cliffs are prevalent. In the Vinh Thanh and Suoi Ca Valley, and along the eastern portion of the AO, the terrain is composed of flat level rice paddies" (HQ 1st Cavalry Division 1966: 4).

This terrain had several important tactical implications for the forthcoming battle. First, observation ranges and fields of fire varied widely – in the valleys both were quite open, but in the mountains they could be measured in a matter of yards. On the flip side, cover and concealment in the mountains was good, whereas in the valleys it was scattered. There were limited LZs, especially along the high ground, and many obstacles for both ground movement and air landing. Tactically, the temptation to

follow accessible routes, such as stream beds, also raised the possibility of walking into ambushes, especially when the routes were surrounded by high ground.

A US reconnaissance outpost on Dong Re Lao mountain scans the A Shau Valley. This image provides a good impression of the challenging nature of the terrain around the valley, the precipitous mountains covered with dense jungle. (Icemanwcs/Wikimedia/ CC BY-SA 3.0)

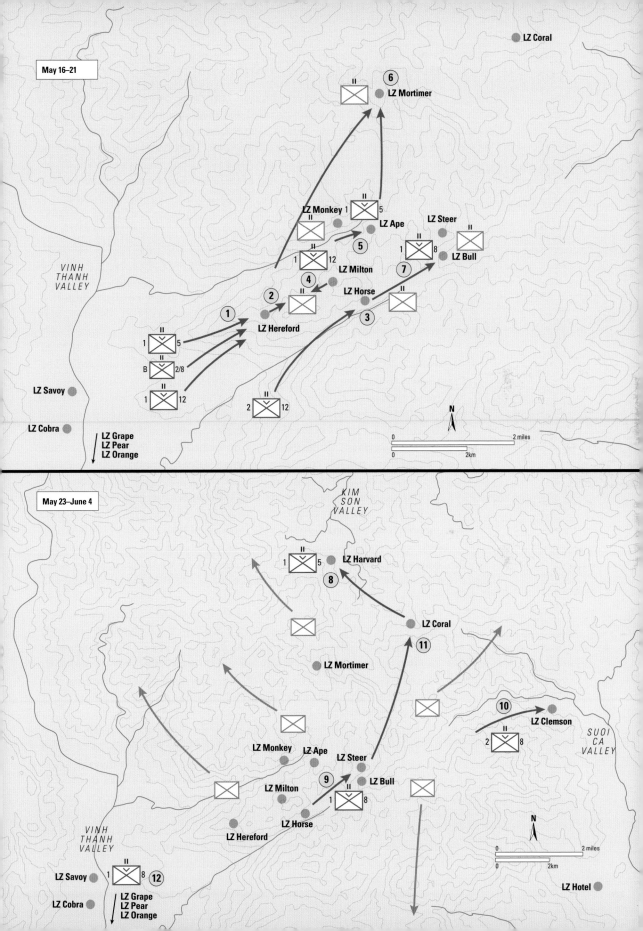

May 16–21

LZ Coral

II ⑥ LZ Mortimer

LZ Monkey 1 II 5
II ⑤ LZ Ape LZ Steer
1 II 12 LZ Milton 1 II 8 LZ Bull
④ LZ Horse ⑦
① ② II LZ Hereford II ③
VINH THANH VALLEY

1 II 5
B II 2/8
1 II 12 2 II 12

LZ Savoy
LZ Cobra

LZ Grape
LZ Pear
LZ Orange

N

0 _____ 2 miles
0 _____ 2km

May 23–June 4

KIM SON VALLEY

1 II 5 LZ Harvard
⑧
LZ Coral
II ⑪

LZ Mortimer

II LZ Clemson
⑩ *SUOI CA VALLEY*
2 II 8

LZ Monkey
LZ Ape
LZ Steer
LZ Milton ⑨ LZ Bull
1 II 8
LZ Horse

LZ Hereford

VINH THANH VALLEY

LZ Savoy 1 II 8 ⑫
LZ Cobra

LZ Grape
LZ Pear
LZ Orange

LZ Hotel

N

0 _____ 2 miles
0 _____ 2km

INTO COMBAT

The action that triggered Operation *Crazy Horse* began on May 16, when Co. B, 2/8 Cav (126 men) was lifted and made a combat assault at 1100hrs into LZ Hereford in the Vinh Thanh Valley, heading out with the intention of sweeping the area around the CIDG camp. (Cos A and C, 2/8 Cav were at the same time conducting a security operation along Highway 19, which ran through An Khe to the eastern end of the Deo Ming Pass.) LZ Hereford was problematic from the start – it only had space to land a single helicopter at a time, thus the assault had an initially slow deployment, a fact that doubtless alerted the PAVN/VC troops in the vicinity.

Once on the ground, the company, commanded by Captain J.D. Coleman, moved up a mountain trail, the men struggling with their heavy packs and weapon loads over rocks, through vegetation, and across gullies and streams. They were alert for contact with the enemy, but might not have suspected that they were actually advancing toward developed PAVN/VC defenses, with about a battalion of enemy troops in the area.

At about 1400hrs, soldiers from the 3d Pltn, walking point, spotted a single VC soldier up ahead, and opened up with their small arms. The response was a torrent of VC return fire, and in seconds the soldiers of Co. B found themselves fighting for their lives. The PAVN/VC soldiers delivered a superb counter-response, aided by their advantage in numbers over the single US company. Entire US squads were nearly wiped out in the first few minutes of the engagement. Immediate reinforcements, requested via frantic radio calls, were not possible because at 1420hrs a violent rainstorm swept in, giving the battlefield a murky, subterranean feel under the vegetation canopy. The PAVN/VC, meanwhile, "hugged" the US troops close; this tactic, plus the limitations imposed by the weather, meant that the beleaguered Co. B had no support from tube artillery and little from Aerial Rocket Artillery (ARA); two helicopter gunships did make a perilous rocket attack in the early evening, helping to suppress some of the enemy fire. All the US troops could do in the end was form a tight defensible perimeter on a section of high ground and attempt to survive the night.

Finally, as the evening rolled in, LZ Hereford received reinforcements from Cos A and C, 1/12 Cav; the former secured LZ Hereford while the latter went and joined up with Co. B, 2/8 Cav, reaching that company at 2230hrs. By this time, Co. B had suffered 20 men killed and 40 wounded. For the PAVN/VC, it had been a good day, although their own casualties were also likely to have been severe, albeit limited by the restrictions on the use of US heavy firepower.

After a restless but relatively quiet night, the firefights resumed at around 0615hrs, at the time Co. B pulled out of the line. The engagement lasted for some two hours, made all the more nail-biting by the fact that the Co. A reinforcements had not brought enough rifle ammunition with them, with the result that the already stretched Co. B was compelled to share. On this day, however, the 1st Air Cav began to scale up its response. Two more battalions were flown into the AO: 1/5th Cav assaulted into LZ Hereford to provide immediate reinforcements there, while 2/12 Cav landed at LZ Horse, about 3.2km (2 miles) to the northeast of Hereford, acting as a blocking force for

A US Army mountaintop firebase, typical of those used to support Air Cav operations in Binh Dinh Province. The howitzers themselves are 105mm M102s: light weapons ideal for underslung helicopter transportation. Note the defensive infantry fighting positions dug into the ground. (© CORBIS/Corbis via Getty Images)

the US troops as they built up strength and pushed out of Hereford. There was fighting throughout the day around Hereford, but eventually it became clear that the PAVN/VC were breaking contact and moving into the difficult mountainous terrain to escape the buildup of US forces.

On the 18th, the US plan was demonstrably beginning to work out. The men of 2/12 Cav found themselves heavily engaged, including by mortars and heavy machine guns, with a large PAVN/VC force, estimated at about company strength. With the assistance of air strikes, the Air Cav company pushed on north, overcoming resistance at an enemy bunker complex, again through use of aircraft-delivered ordnance. By the end of the day, 2/12 Cav had linked up with Co. B, 1/5 Cav, which had experienced only light resistance during the day's advance. The following day, both 2/12 Cav and 1/5 Cav continued to sweep through their immediate area of operations. It was a day of light contact, but there were grisly indications all around that the PAVN/VC were taking heavy losses. The two battalions continued this activity on the 20th, but during this day 2/12 Cav was relieved by 1/8 Cav,

Firefight, Vinh Thanh Valley, May 21, 1966

Here we see troops from Co. B, 1/8 Cav, engaged in a ferocious firefight in the jungle-covered mountains bordering the Vinh Thanh Valley. The soldiers have just been ambushed by seasoned troops of the 8th Bn, 22d PAVN Regt, from ambush positions prepared in advance, with fields of fire looking down over the Americans' line of advance. American troops responding to the attack follow the immediate-action drill, moving to cover and putting down heavy suppressive fire. The M60 machine-gunner plays a crucial role here, as the 7.62×51mm rounds have greater penetrative power than the M16 assault rifles used by the other men. One American soldier has already been hit by incoming fire, and is being dragged to safety by another soldier; throughout the action on May 21–22, Air Cav infantry demonstrated extreme bravery in not only rescuing their wounded compatriots, but also collecting their dead from the battlefield. During many such firefights in jungle terrain, it would often be difficult just to see the enemy let alone accurately target him. This was often the reason why American troops would halt and call in air strikes, but in this particular action the US and PAVN soldiers fought at close quarters.

which had flown out from the division base area. This deployment would lead to renewed heavy fighting, and a demonstration that the PAVN/VC were still out there in force.

On the 21st, Cos B and C, 1/8 Cav found themselves moving through the twilit world of the jungled mountains, as they conducted their sweep up a trail in the valley northwest of LZ Horse. They were primarily using the stream beds for movement, and it was likely that they were being watched. At one point, two enemy soldiers were spotted up among the trees, but they sprinted off before they could be engaged. Then, at about 1547hrs, Co. B was suddenly subjected to an explosive ambush, which included not only small-arms fire but also heavy-machine-gun fire from 12.7mm and 7.62mm weapons. Later intelligence indicated that the soldiers behind the ambush belonged to the 8th Bn, 22d PAVN Regt, 601st PAVN Division. After taking heavy casualties from the initial bursts of fire, the men of Co. B eventually recovered their orientation and, in a remarkable display of necessary courage, turned the tables on their attackers, and assaulted and overran the PAVN positions. Second Lieutenant William L. McCarron led the 2d Pltn of Co. B and took a dramatic personal role in attacking the enemy positions. He located an enemy machine gun about 23m (25yd) away, set by the side of a trail and well camouflaged in the undergrowth. Recognizing that the weapon posed a direct threat to Co. B's assault forward on the bunker complex, he drew a grenade, pulled the pin, and hurled it forward. At the moment it detonated, he leapt up and sprinted forward, running downhill toward the position and firing with his M16 assault rifle. He shot three PAVN soldiers as he advanced; the seriously wounded PAVN machine-gunner attempted to grab his personal weapon, but McCarron finished him off before he could reach it. Looking up, McCarron then spotted, and shot, another PAVN soldier who was approaching the position carrying spare machine-gun ammunition. He took the soldier's SKS rifle, slung it on his back, and advanced toward another PAVN bunker position, first throwing a grenade through the entrance then spraying the interior with M16 fire, after which the bunker was silent (McCarron 2015: 9–10).

All around McCarron, the other members of Co. B were attacking with similar ferocity, hitting the PAVN positions with M16 and M60 fire,

William McCarron was typical of the young officers who served in the 1st Air Cav during the 1960s. He was born in Kelty in Fife, Scotland in 1940, but in March 1964, now a US citizen, he volunteered for service in the US Army and received a commission as a 2d lieutenant in December that year. Between 1966 and 1970 he served two tours of Vietnam. The first was from March 1966 to March 1967, in which he served in Co. B, 1/8 Cav, a period of service that included Operation *Crazy Horse* and many other operations that involved the battalion. His second tour ran from November 1969 through November 1970, with Advisory Team 72, Vinh Binh Province, IV CTZ. He rose to the rank of captain during his time in Vietnam, his leadership roles including platoon commander, executive officer, and acting company commander in a combat rifle company, and, with the rank of captain, Province Senior Phoenix Coordinator and Assistant Province Phoenix Coordinator. His citations and awards for service in Vietnam include the Silver Star and Purple Heart.

grenades, and 40mm M79 rocket-propelled grenades. The danger was not just coming from ground level: the PAVN/VC were adept at placing snipers high up in the trees, concealed in the dense foliage. Combined with the threat from ground-emplaced mines, booby traps, and punji pits (traps lined with sharpened bamboo punji sticks), this sniper activity demonstrated how the North Vietnamese troops were adept at placing their enemy under multilevel tension.

Progressively, every bunker was cleared by the US soldiers, often at great personal cost. McCarron noted that the PAVN force had to be taking unsustainable levels of casualties, as by early evening the volumes of incoming fire were starting to diminish. Furthermore, the US troops were starting to take their toll of evidently fleeing enemy troops. As the pressure eased, and as night fell under the drum of heavy rainfall, the Air Cav soldiers gathered their dead and wounded and established a defensive perimeter, which they guarded nervously throughout the night. To give the US troops some visibility, distant artillery fired illumination rounds throughout the night.

Although there were some minor probes of the perimeter, the night passed largely without incident, and in the morning CH-47As arrived overhead and winched up the dead and wounded. (McCarron makes the interesting procedural note that the CH-47As first made a supply drop, which included chainsaws so that the troops on the ground could cut a clearing for the evacuation.) Eventually, Co. B was airlifted out from LZ Horse to LZ Colt,

General Nguyen Chi Thanh (1914–67) was one of the architects of the PAVN/VC strategy in South Vietnam. Born in Thura Thien Province, he became actively involved with the Indochinese Communist Party during the 1930s, and during the French Indochina War (1945–54) became a PAVN general, but subsequently also held high political office, being elected to the Central Committee and appointed to the Politburo and the Secretariat during the early 1960s. He returned to military command in 1965 within COSVN, informing both PAVN and VC tactics, including urging troops to "Hold the enemy's belt" to obviate their firepower advantage. Thanh died in Hanoi on July 7, 1967, either from a heart attack (according to North Vietnamese sources), or as a result of US bombing (American sources).

from where the company continued to conduct offensive patrols, despite what its personnel had just been through. Sniper and small-unit actions remained a threat, and Co. B's commander, Captain Roy D. Martin, suffered a serious leg wound from a sniper shot. The final tally of the fighting on the 21st was 11 dead from Co. B and two dead from Co. C.

After the harrowing clash on the 21st, the next day was relatively quiet as the 1st Bde continued its sweep operations. There were just a handful of small-arms clashes as the US companies moved around the territory, the advancing troops closing up to blocking positions. The PAVN/VC were now obviously operating on weakened legs, based on the sporadic nature of the contact. At 2250hrs, for example, a PAVN/VC mortar team put down 16 rounds of mortar fire on LZ Cobra, now the position of 2/8 Cav. The fire was ineffective, however, and no casualties were reported.

During May 24–31, the battle entered a new phase as the bulk of the activity focused on the US units establishing and maintaining their blocking positions while the full weight of US air power was brought in to pound suspected enemy positions, including heavyweight strikes by B-52 bombers. Divisional artillery also targeted suspected egress points; multiple FSBs had been established around the AO as the weather became more amenable to airlifts. The after-action report for May 29–30 noted:

> The 1st Brigade continued to block routes of egress from the AO with four US battalions, one air cavalry squadron (-), one ROK battalion and ARVN Task Force Bravo. Three CIDG companies continued to search to encircled land mass with light to heavy contact during the period. The CIDG were joined by part of one US battalion in search operations on 30 May. TAC strikes and artillery fires were used extensively on VC locations. (HQ 1st Cavalry Division 1966: 8)

From June 1 to the operation's conclusion on June 5, the brigade, and also the ROK Army and ARVN forces assigned to the operation, continued search operations throughout the now bomb-blasted territory. For the Air Cav soldiers, the levels of contact now remained light; CIDG troops involved in the action experienced some heavier contacts during patrols.

On June 5, Operation *Crazy Horse* was concluded, with 2/8 Cav, 1/12 Cav, and the ROK Army battalions airlifted back to the base areas, while 1/8 Cav took an overland route. It was now time to take stock of the cost and results of the operation. In terms of the human cost, total casualties for the US forces were 440 men, including 83 KIA and 1 MIA. The ROK Army, CIDG, and ARVN units had 50 casualties in total. These were appreciable losses, and added to the increasing tally of dead and wounded suffered by the 1st Air Cav during 1966. As usual, the total number of PAVN/VC dead and wounded was open to some measure of both estimation and "creative accounting." The actual body count was 507, 350 of which were claimed by the 1st Air Cav, plus a further 381 estimated. Adding in other figures, the likely total casualties, including wounded, were likely in the region of 1,200, which represented another serious blow against PAVN/VC strength in South Vietnam.

Operational details of PAVN/VC tactics and command during Operation *Crazy Horse* are, as in many other battles, scarce or absent. Throughout the

operation, the PAVN/VC troops once again demonstrated their confidence and ability in setting and executing ambushes, and in slipping away once casualties and US firepower rendered the contact a futile endeavor. More revelations about their field operations lay in documents and materiel discovered in the aftermath of battle. McCarron noted that during his platoon's movement back to LZ Horse, they came across an extensive PAVN/VC base camp, which included latrines, concealed cooking fires, and sleeping areas (McCarron 2015: 11); he judged the base area sufficient to hold a battalion-strength unit. The 1st Air Cav tally of materiel captured included nine crew-served weapons, 82 personal weapons, 26,300 rounds of small-arms ammunition, 76 rounds of mortar ammunition, 166 grenades, two radios, 90,025lb of rice, and 20,875lb of salt – evidently, the PAVN/VC troops were planning on an extended campaign.

A white phosphorus (WP) bomb explodes in a South Vietnamese village, dropped by an A-1E Skyraider. Air support of this kind was crucial to the successful outcome of many Air Cav operations. White phosphorus munitions caused fires over a widespread area, but were also used to mark targets for following aircraft armed with napalm or high-explosive ordnance. (Larry Burrows/ The LIFE Picture Collection via Getty Images)

The "Miscellaneous" category in the after-action report provides a further window into the activities and equipment of the PAVN/VC units: "10 mortar fuses, 54 blasting caps, 1 detonator, 5 sections – Bangalore Torpedo, 30 – ½lb blocks explosive, 2 pair binoculars, 2 compasses, 8 signal flares, 240 lbs medical supplies, 260 lbs documents, 1 typewriter, 2 bicycles, 20 shovels, 360 uniforms, and 106 packs" (HQ 1st Cavalry Division 1966: 9). The large number of uniforms is particular interesting – evidently the PAVN/VC units were expecting more recruits. Certainly, despite the apparent success of battles such as Operation *Crazy Horse*, with their body counts disproportionately weighted toward the North Vietnamese, the PAVN and VC were not having a problem in continuing their prosecution of the war.

Tam Quan

December 6–20, 1967

BACKGROUND TO BATTLE

The Vietnam War involved constant US attempts at pacification, the battle often being fought over the same ground repeatedly. One of the central problems for the US forces in Vietnam was quite simply that the PAVN and VC would steadily trickle back into areas that had been ostensibly cleared during search-and-destroy operations, once the US troops had left the AO and returned to their bases. This rhythm – demoralizing for the Americans

An unidentified soldier with the 1st Air Cav presents a wary expression, as he levels his XM16E1 assault rifle. He has a single water canteen on his hip. During long operations, soldiers would usually carry about a gallon of water in such containers, distributed between belt and backpack. (Christopher Jensen/Getty Images)

A truly impressive image of massed helicopters flying over an LZ during Operation *Pershing*, 1967. Landing such a volume of aviation was a challenge, as each helicopter typically needed a space 20m (66ft) wide and 75m (246ft) long to put down safely. (Patrick Christain/Getty Images)

and costly for the PAVN – characterized the Vietnam War in the second half of the 1960s.

The last battle in this volume, the battle of Tam Quan in December 1967, falls into this pattern. It was fought on the Bong Son Plain, which had already been the scene of much fighting in Operation *Masher*. On February 12, 1967, the US Army launched Operation *Pershing*, another intensive effort to quash the PAVN/VC presence in Binh Dinh Province. The key focus of this operation was, once again, to clear the Bong Son Plain and then the An Lao Valley, an operational AO dominated by the 3d PAVN Division. It would develop into one of the longest regional campaigns of the war: Operation *Pershing* ran until January 19, 1968. The battle of Tam Quan was just one element of that action and, as it turned out, the biggest action of the campaign.

In 1967, the PAVN escalated the infiltration of units into South Vietnam, in readiness for what would become the Tet Offensive, not least within Binh Dinh Province. During late November and early December 1967, intelligence reports indicated that the 22d PAVN Regt was especially active, with potential attacks being planned between Tam Quan on the eastern coast and Bong Son. Fueling concern, PAVN attacks in the area began to increase during early December, and there were even reports that the 22d PAVN Regt HQ had actually moved into Tam Quan. Both the 1st Air Cav and local ARVN units upped their reconnaissance efforts, and on December 6 a reconnaissance helicopter of 1/9 Cav detected a radio antenna projecting from the roof of a hooch in Dai Dong, a village just to the south of Tam Quan. Acting quickly, the 1st Air Cav sent in two platoons of troops to sweep through the village later in the afternoon. What they discovered, following the first landing there at 1630hrs, was a major enemy concentration of the 22d PAVN Regt that quickly had them pinned down with defensive fire. Reinforcements flew in 25 minutes later, in the form of a weapons platoon, but they also were fixed into position by an unequal firefight.

The 40mm M42 "Duster" SPAAG vehicle was used in support of Air Cav operations around Tam Quan. Its main weapon was the 40mm M2A1 twin antiaircraft gun with 336 rounds. (From the Robert L. Drieslein Collection (COLL/5643) at the Archives Branch, Marine Corps History Division/Wikimedia/Public Domain)

It was this initial action, which confirmed the intelligence suspicions, that triggered the "battle of Tam Quan," although much of it occurred in Dai Dong village. This would not purely be a 1st Air Cav operation. It would also include armor from the 1/50 Mechanized Infantry Regt plus soldiers from the 3d and 4th Marine Bns, 40th ARVN Regiment. The operational objectives were clear:

MISSION: Fix and destroy the 22d NVA Regiment.

CONCEPT OF OPERATIONS: The 1st Bde utilizes mechanized forces for armored protection and firepower and organic maneuver units to overrun and destroy the enemy once he is fixed [in position]. All available air and artillery fires are utilized to drive the enemy from his prepared positions or to destroy him in his positions prior to all attacks. Use of riot control agent CS emphasized in the preps in conjunction with artillery and air fires. Other allied forces and organic and attached units used on the periphery of contact areas to inhibit the escape of the enemy. Detailed planning and execution of artillery blocking fires, fires in the objective area and illumination for night operations is necessary. Contact with the enemy must be maintained but if lost immediate pursuit must be executed by fire, aerial surveillance and by maneuver units. Thorough police of all contact areas is essential following the defeat and expulsion of the enemy. Priority of all fires to the attacking units. (US Army 1968: 4)

In contrast to the previous battles, the use of armored assets would play a more central role, which combined with artillery and air power would make this a true combined-arms action. For the PAVN forces, the initial contact on

December 7 must have alerted them to the fact that a major defensive battle was on its way, doubtless delivered by air assault. After so many furtive search-and-destroy actions in 1965–67, the impending battle promised a far more conventional clash of arms.

UH-1Ds prepare to move Air Cav soldiers between LZs during a combat operation. When the helicopters were moving small, important units such as headquarters staff or key support personnel, the men would often be divided between different helicopters to avoid the loss of all or most of the unit should the helicopter be shot down. (© Hulton-Deutsch Collection/CORBIS/Corbis via Getty Images)

Soldiers from the 1st Air Cav stand guard over an LZ waiting for the second wave of assault helicopters to land. They have marked the LZ using smoke grenades as markers to guide the incoming pilots. (NARA 100310308/ Wikimedia/Public Domain)

1 December 6: Elements of the 22d and 28th PAVN regiments occupy defensive positions around Tam Quan, Dai Dong, Binh Phu, and Truong Lam.

2 1800hrs, December 6: 1/8 Cav makes an air assault into positions around Dai Dong. The battalion faces elements of the 22d PAVN Regt, which are distributed around the Tam Quan area.

3 Evening, December 6: Elements of the 40th ARVN Regiment make a sweep around the east of the AO to establish blocking positions.

4 0815hrs, December 7: 1/8 Cav completes its movement into the landing zone at Dai Dong, making heavy contacts with PAVN forces.

5 December 7: During the day, elements of the 40th ARVN Regiment make assaults above and below Dai Dong, protecting the flanks of the US operation and inhibiting PAVN/VC movement out of the area of operations.

6 0915hrs, December 7: 2/8 Cav makes an air assault to the east of Dai Dong, establishing a US blocking position.

7 0745hrs, December 8: Co. C, 1/8 Cav air assaults into positions around Dai Dong to relieve Co. B, 1/8 Cav from the area.

8 December 8: Co. D, 1/50 Mech provides armored support for the US infantry assaulting through Dai Dong.

9 December 9: 2/8 Cav continues to make sweeps in the south of the AO, attempting to pursue what intelligence reports indicate might be the 9th Bn, 22d PAVN Regt.

10 1541hrs, December 9: Co. C, 1/12 Cav air assault into positions around Truong Lam, preventing the PAVN from using the sea as an escape route.

11 December 10: By this stage in the battle, the PAVN forces are beginning to disperse throughout the AO, although some units will still fight defensive battles in certain locations.

12 December 11–14: US and ARVN forces make a concerted push to the north through the AO, driving up to positions around LZ Loboy.

13 0719hrs, December 15: 1/12 Cav is air assaulted into Truong Lam and makes heavy contact with elements of the 22d PAVN Regt. The US battalion later receives support from 1/50 Mech.

14 December 19–20: ARVN units and 2/8 Cav make a concerted push in the south of the AO, neutralizing PAVN elements in the area and bringing the operation to an end.

15 December 20: By the final stage of the battle, the surviving PAVN units have broken down into small groups of soldiers, using minor escape-and-evasion routes to flee the US offensive, heading toward the jungle-covered mountains of the interior.

Battlefield environment

The general battlefield environment of the Bong Son Plain has already been described in the analysis of Operation *Masher*. For the clash around Tam Quan, the fighting would be confined to the relatively narrow coastal strip, which consisted of sandy beaches immediately on the coastline, open fields, rice paddies, and palm groves. Hamlets and domestic dwellings punctuated the landscape, with the unfortunate consequence that many civilian dwellings were directly in fields of fire. In Operations *Masher* and *Crazy Horse*, inclement weather played its part in the development of the battle. At this time of the year, however, the Bong Son Plain was just coming out of its monsoon season, and the weather in December was typically sunny and pleasant, which meant that there would be few restrictions on the use of air power.

1st Air Cav helicopters conduct a mountaintop resupply mission in February 1966. The high operational demand placed upon helicopters in the division meant that typically only 60–70 percent of the total aviation assets were available for missions at any one time, the rest undergoing maintenance and repair. (© Wally McNamee/CORBIS/Corbis via Getty Images)

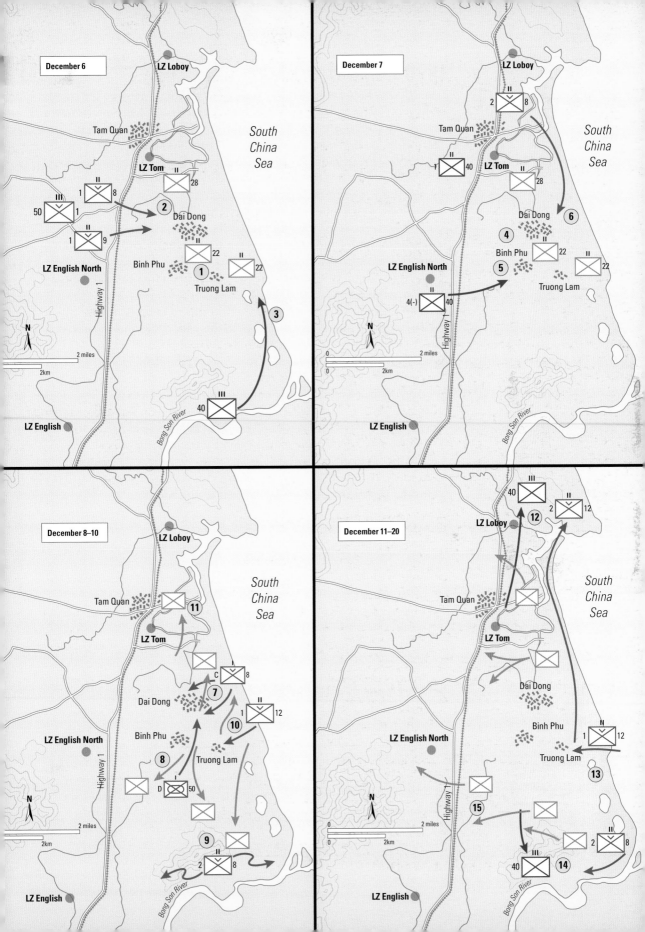

INTO COMBAT

The PAVN troops around Dai Dong were waiting. Many of the troops were occupying emplaced positions, often concealed in dense undergrowth to create a patchwork of ambush positions. The 1st Bde of the Air Cav, meanwhile, attempted to use its airmobile capabilities to reinforce rapidly the beleaguered men of 1/9 Cav, who were literally fighting for their lives. At 1800hrs, Co. B, 1/8 Cav was air assaulted into the area, supported by an ACAV (Armored Cavalry Assault Vehicle platoon) from Co. A, 1/50 Mech, which moved in overland. Both of the platoons first landed in the area were extracted successfully, but the cavalry soldiers were surprised by the intensity of the resistance, with both infantry and armor taking casualties. Combat had largely ceased by 2200hrs, but the US artillery kept up its drumbeat throughout the night, pounding potential escape routes for the enemy.

The chief objective now for the Air Cav was to ramp up superiority in firepower and personnel at Dai Dong. To this end, at 0815hrs the next day, Co. A, 1/8 Cav was air assaulted into the AO, with Cos B and C, 2/8 Cav being deployed at 0915hrs farther to the south and fanning out to restrict the enemy's escape routes to the east. Substantial amounts of armor were also pouring into the battle zone, including another ACAV platoon, two sections of 40mm M42 "Duster" Self-Propelled Anti-Aircraft Gun (SPAAG) vehicles (each mounting a 40mm automatic cannon), flamethrower APCs, and also D-7 bulldozers, which could crush or smother enemy strongpoints.

The assault to the east by 1/8 Cav on the morning of the 7th was stunning in its intensity. A former soldier of the 1/8 Cav, Richard Dieterle, noted the chaos and noise of battle from the moment of touchdown:

> We were still moving at a good clip, when all of a sudden the noise level doubled. A B-40 rocket blew up about 5 yards to my right just when I happened to be looking in that direction. One of the men of the 4th Platoon dropped with shrapnel in his ankle. While they were helping him to his feet, the men on the APCs began to get hit right and left. The assault completely stalled. Suddenly it seemed as if the world had slowed down and I was high on some unheard of drug. The whole world moved in slow motion. At the time, I thought I must be the only person in history to have this odd neural reaction, but otherwise, I felt perfectly self-possessed. I snapped out of it like the pop of a bubble. The APCs had come to a grinding halt. We edged up to ours to increase our cover. By now every gunner on the APC to our right had been hit and had gotten off their track. The APC on our right was now only about 5 yards away. One of the Brothers courageously mounted the right rear machine gun, despite the fate of its previous owner. I then swung my head slightly to the left and, as my eyes swept over the APC to our right, I could see Tewksbury, a member of the 4th platoon, jump up on the side of the APC. He was trying to get up there so that he could man the .50 caliber machine gun. He was short and heavy for his size, and when he got himself atop the beast, he stood facing the enemy with his back to the gun. As I stood there watching him I saw the cloth of his shirt ripple twice in rapid succession as two bullets punctured his heart. He leaned forward almost 90°, then with a slow clockwise motion dropped over the side of the APC like a bag of flour. (Dieterle 2020)

A .50-caliber M55 quad weapon system puts down heavy fire in support of operations by Co. D, 1/7 Cav. The effective firing range of this weapon was about 1.6km (1 mile), but its maximum range could extend more than three times this distance. (US Army Heritage and Education Center/Wikimedia/Public Domain)

Such was the violence of the defense that the US attack ground to halt. The infantry and armor paused and pulled back, giving a bit more ground for artillery, ARA, and tactical air strikes. The artillery also dropped CS shells, the clouds of anti-riot agent causing intense respiratory and ocular irritation.

At 1406hrs, Cos A and B, 1/8 Cav renewed their attack, supported by even more armor from 1/50 Mech, including flamethrower tanks, which the after-action report noted were particularly useful in burning up enemy bunkers and trenches. Armored bulldozers took out several more positions, and also constructed a causeway across rice paddies to facilitate APC movement. Meanwhile, 2/8 Cav was operating farther out to the west, just to the west of Highway 1. They, along with ARVN forces, provided screening operations and their levels of contact were far lighter than those experienced by 1/8 Cav to the east. The after-action report did note, however, that "At 1645 hours, the CP of C Company was pinned down by intense automatic weapons fire while crossing a rice paddy vicinity BS 922072. The CP was finally extracted at 1900 hours and joined the rest of the company at their night location" (US Army 1968: 5).

On December 8, the situation for the PAVN defenders was becoming increasingly bleak. During the morning, many of them were driven from their bunkers by choking clouds of CS gas, only to be killed by artillery and air strikes as they emerged into the open air. In one incident alone, some 23 PAVN soldiers died by this tactic. Co. C, 1/8 Cav had been airlifted in at 0745hrs to relieve Co. B. Dieterle notes that shortly after the new company was landed, American aerial gunships (likely AC-47Ds) mistook the unit for enemy troops (having not been informed of their deployment), and hit them with heavy aerial weaponry, killing one soldier and injuring 14. Despite this early setback, Cos A and C, 1/8 Cav, gained further traction over the tactical situation, pushing out to the east and north in coordination with Co. D, 1/50 Mech, against steadily reducing resistance. Often they would find that the artillery and air strikes had done their work for them, wiping out many of the defenders' positions.

By midday, much of the armor had been deployed outside of the immediate combat area and adopted a defensive readiness. Meanwhile, 2/8 Cav went searching for 9th Bn, 22d PAVN Regt, which had been reported in the area, but found nothing. The 40th ARVN Regt, however, did make contact with 8th Bn, 22d PAVN Regt, and there was some further heavy fighting.

December 9 was a day of consolidation in Dai Dong. An early-morning artillery and CS barrage prepped the enemy positions once again, and the Air Cav troops and mechanized elements made a final sweep through the village, reaching the southern edge with almost no resistance. Given this success, there was some rearrangement of the forces in the AO. One change was the formation of Task Force "Dolphin," composed of 1/50 Mech (-) operating with Co. B, 1/8 Cav and Co. C, 1/12 Cav, which had just been airlifted in from Dak To. Much of the fighting on this day was confined to the ARVN's sectors, as it was attacked by elements of the 8th Bn, 22d PAVN Regt.

On December 10 there came a new development and fighting. In the early morning the commanding officer of the 40th ARVN Regt reported that civilians had been seen running from the village of Truong Lam, just to the east of Dai Dong and nestling on the shoreline of the South China Sea. This activity likely indicated an enemy presence in the village; the civilians were either expelled from their homes, or simply did not want to stay to be caught in a major battle. Co. D, 1/12 Cav and Co. B, 1/50 Mech maneuvered onto the village, and were joined by Co. B, 1/12 Cav, which assaulted into a nearby LZ at 0825hrs. Inside the village were elements of the 7th Bn, 22d PAVN Regt, which had likely been retreating from the fighting at Dai Dong. The enemy presence was confirmed at 1055hrs, when approaching US forces came under extremely intense fire. The three US units responded with a coordinated envelopment, with Co. B, 1/12 Cav attacking around the western flank of the village, while Co. C, 1/12 Cav made an air assault to close the left flank, and the armor fixed the PAVN troops in the center. Still, the PAVN in the village fought stubbornly for their lives, three major attacks by the US forces during the afternoon making progress in grinding forward against trenchant resistance. Only the following morning, after another effective artillery and CS strike, did the combined Air Cav/Mech force overwhelm the remaining elements of resistance.

The battle of Tam Quan was now entering a phase similar to previous operations, with the Air Cav making a series of widening search and blocking actions in the effort to trap and destroy the PAVN forces as they attempted to disperse, escape, and survive. The 1/8 Cav had been sent out west of Highway 1 onto the Bong Son Plain in pursuit of the 9th Bn, 22d PAVN Regt, although this enemy unit remained elusive. Meanwhile, 2/8 Cav was in positions to block escape routes to the Cay Giep mountains. On the 12th, an ARVN Marine Task Force Alpha, TF Dolphin, and Task Force 1/12 Cav began pursuing the 22d PAVN Regt directly to the north. They did make contact in the late morning, and this pocket of resistance was soon snuffed out.

For the next two days, the PAVN/VC forces largely seemed to have ceased significant combat operations. There were some relatively minor engagements, but these were largely small-unit clashes. Much of the work on

A job not for the faint-hearted – a US soldier is lowered by colleagues into an enemy tunnel complex during a search-and-destroy operation. A common PAVN tactic was to unleash an ambush and then retreat underground to sit out the near-inevitable shelling or air strike. (NARA 530613/ Wikimedia/Public Domain)

December 13–14 consisted of winkling out bunkers and fighting positions. Then, on December 15, intelligence was received that there were major elements of the 22d PAVN Regt just to the west of Truong Lam, thus Co. D, 1/12 Cav was air assaulted into the region, joining Cos B and C, 1/12 Cav in the operation. It turned out to be the beginning of a large-scale two-day clash. The after-action report evokes the complex coordinated maneuvers performed by the US units:

> D 1-12 air assaulted vicinity BS 922052 from LZ ENGLISH at 0719 hours and all companies began the search for the enemy. At 0810 hours contact was initiated by C-12. All companies began to close into the area of contact. A request was forwarded to the 1st ACD for an additional Mech Company from 1-50 Mech and approval was granted. C-12 moved to vicinity BS 918053 and was heavily engaged. B 1-12 moved west to vicinity BS 921055 and was in moderate contact. D 1-12 moved southwest and then to the north executing a flanking movement and was in light to heavy contacts throughout the movement. The company succeeded in penetrating the enemy positions to vicinity BS 913054. [...] Intense tactical airstrikes and an artillery preparation were used in an attempt to neutralize enemy positions and at 1530 hours A (-) 1-50 Mech and C 1-12 Cav attack to the north. This attack was repulsed by savage enemy resistance and all elements pulled back to break contact and allow heavy artillery fires to soften the enemy positions. By 1745 hours contact was broken and all elements were in their night defensive positions. (US Army 1968: 8)

At the same time as this engagement was occurring, 1/8 Cav, 2/8 Cav, and the 40th ARVN Regt were being moved to blocking positions around the north, south, and west of the immediate combat area.

The next day, the 16th, the combined cavalry and armor once again made an offensive sweep through Truong Lam, attacking after six tactical air strikes, a CS strike, plus the standard 10-minute preparatory pounding by artillery. This time, the village offered up little in the way of resistance, and from December 16–18 the bulk of activity was spent in pursuit and sweep operations to try to make contact again with the 22d PAVN Regt, whatever condition that was now in. There were few sightings, let alone contacts, but that changed on the 19th, when an intelligence report placed the enemy regiment (or at least an aerial leading down into a large bunker complex), between Highway 1 and the coastline, just below the Bong Son River. Co. D, 2/8 Cav was quickly air assaulted into the area, and the enemy presence was confirmed by the immediate resistance on the ground. The cavalry troops halted to allow tactical air support and artillery to do their preparatory work.

The after-action report noted that an airborne Psychological Warfare Team first made an orbit over the area, using loudspeakers to tell any civilians in the village to get out while they could. The results of this action are unclear; what is not is that the bunker complex was then wiped out by six heavy air strikes by 1700hrs, the report noting that the US Air Force aircraft delivered their ordnance with "pinpoint accuracy" (US Army 1968: 10). The cavalry then established 360-degree blocking positions around the village, with Co. D, 2/8 Cav on the east, Co. B, 2/8 Cav to the south, Co. C, 2/8 Cav to the west, and Co. D, 1/8 Cav to the southeast; the Bong Son River itself provided a physical blocking position to the north. Throughout the day, artillery hit the positions within the ring established by the cavalry. As an indication of the effectiveness of the hammering, at several points during the day enemy soldiers were observed, in desperation, attempting to cross the river, and were killed by artillery and small-arms fire.

With the last pockets of resistance quashed, it was now time for the battle of Tam Quan to cease, which it did on December 20. The after-action data illustrate the levels to which heavy firepower played a key role in the battle. Total expenditure of artillery shells was 45,406, to which we can add air-dropped ordnance: 302 M82 High Drag bombs, 225 M117 General Purpose bombs, 116 napalm bombs, and 29,400 rounds of 20mm cannon ammunition. Once again, the PAVN had suffered severe materiel and human losses. The former included 45 bunkers and 118 other military structures destroyed, while total casualties were 650 dead (inflicted by the combined US and ARVN efforts) and 32 captured (US only). The Americans had lost 58 dead and 250 wounded.

The battle of Tam Quan, as the accounts above demonstrate, truly fulfilled the intended combat efficiency of the combined-arms principle. The "Commander's Analysis" section in the after-action report, written by Colonel Donald V. Rattan, the CO of 1st Bde, duly noted that

> The victory is equally shared in the outstanding and courageous participation by allies, other services and other units not normally found operating with the 1st Bde. The force that was molded on the field of battle during the period 6–20 December 1967 was an unbeatable combination of air, land and sea elements fully supported by outstanding combat support and unit of all types and missions. (US Army 1968: 8)

Analysis

"Unbeatable." That word, used in Colonel Rattan's summary of the battle of Tam Quan, could be applied to the 1st Air Cav in 1966–68. The terrible Air Cav losses in the battle of Ia Drang in November 1965 had shown the US military that there was no ground for complacency, even against an enemy who was deemed to be inferior in technology and training. Consequently, the increasingly refined combination of airmobile maneuverability, heavy support fire (from both air and artillery), and overwhelming logistical power meant that in every battle, taken as a whole, the 1st Air Cav always came out on top – at least when measured by body count and the fact that many PAVN units were left combat-ineffective or were destroyed altogether, temporarily at least.

August 1972. Young PAVN women carry artillery shells to the front line. At this point, the PAVN was engaged in another major conventional offensive, known as the Easter Offensive (March–October 1972). Although the onslaught did not result in outright victory, the PAVN secured more territory in South Vietnam and further weakened the ARVN. (VAN BANG/AFP via Getty Images)

What we cannot say, however, is that the PAVN and VC Main Force were easy opponents to fight. Indeed, many major historical studies of the Vietnam War have concluded that General Westmoreland's body count metric was a truly poor way to judge the overall progress of the war; arguably, each battle was US tactical victory but a strategic defeat, and in the end the strategy counted for more than the tactics.

Even tactically, however, the PAVN was an opponent to be respected. For a start, we have to acknowledge that for much of the time the PAVN was simply hard to find. Their tactics of constant movement, concealment, and underground living meant that for every hour the US soldiers spent locked in combat, many more hours were spent simply searching or pursuing, often without fruitful conclusion. When the PAVN did fight, however, for the duration of the engagement that stayed a small-unit encounter, fought principally with small arms and light weapons, they could more than hold their own, especially if they could initiate the action through an ambush, a tactic in which they demonstrated talent. Until the post-US years, there are no real examples of PAVN troops winning entire battles or campaigns, but there are many, many examples of the PAVN beating, for a time at least, individual platoons or companies in close-quarter firefights.

In terms of the Air Cav, and indeed all airmobile infantry in the Vietnam War, a distinct challenge for the PAVN was the helicopter and the aerial assault, an aviation element that it simply did not possess itself. Thus they devoted some attention to antiaircraft tactics, as a 1967 RAND Corporation study acknowledged. The study was primarily focused on VC units operating in the Mekong Delta, but the context, and the quoted sources within the passage, indicate that this was general knowledge throughout PAVN and VC forces:

> The Viet Cong perceived the helicopter as a major problem and in 1962–63 the Liberation Army did a number of studies of its combat experience. The Army reacted by setting up organic anti-aircraft units and by experimenting with different tactics for shooting down helicopters.
> *Through a period of hunting down helicopters, the Army and the people of South Vietnam have grasped the technical nature of the helicopters and devised different methods of shooting at the helicopters.*
> For the period covered in this study, 1964–66, the "best" methods for downing helicopters have been incorporated into training and field manuals. For example one source states that
> *... "artillery specialists," using 12.7mm weapons at battalion level, used a formula to compute their gun-laying patterns. [All he knew] of the equations was that they were based on the speed and altitude of the attacking aircraft and the muzzle velocity of the defending weapons.*
> *Anti-aircraft techniques were much simpler at company level where the aiming point depended on the type and speed of the plane itself, for example, one was to shoot one half to one full body length ahead of the helicopter with the inclination of the weapon at such an angle that when the helicopter ran into the bullets, they would be striking around the general area of the engine.*
> In fact one document lists the various techniques of shooting down aircraft with infantry weapons; it gives an approximation formula for computing the distance

that a target must be led to achieve a hit, and it presents a firing table based on the formula for different types of aircraft. Such firing tables occur frequently in the documents we have. (Anderson 1967: 55–56)

During Operation *Pershing* in July 1969, a soldier from 9 Cav searches a destroyed VC supply cave in the An Lao Valley, a place that was a PAVN/VC stronghold for much of the Vietnam War. (NARA 530615/Wikimedia/Public Domain)

From this explanation, it is clear that the PAVN soldiers were no strangers to exploring the science of warfare to improve their tactics against US forces and the ARVN. During Operation *Masher*, for example, the helicopter assault phase was very roughly handled, with some units actually unable to touch down at the LZ and many helicopters either damaged or brought down. Were it not for the fact that the Air Cav could, once the PAVN LZ defenders had basically identified their positions by opening fire, bring down hell and thunder in terms of suppressive firepower, many LZs would have become permanently inaccessible.

The PAVN was perfectly capable of conducting offensive operations, especially if it had the benefit of advanced planning and a defined target, such as a military base. The war against the Air Cav was different, however, in that it was largely defensive, responding to the sudden ingress of large airmobile units on search-and-destroy operations. Against this tactic, the PAVN had three essential means of defense: first, inflict attrition at/around the LZs and in subsequent ambushes; second, fight the US troops from pre-prepared defensive positions; and third, escape the tightening American trap or, *in extremis*, attempt to hide. In essence, the PAVN's biggest enemy during these encounters was time: the longer the battle went on, the more US firepower would orientate onto their positions. From the moment the first shot was fired, the clock was ticking against the PAVN.

Reading through many of the US after-action reports, one can detect a background frustration embedded in the "lessons learned" sections. A common cause of handwringing was to find ways in which to trap the enemy more efficiently between sweeps and blocking movements, preventing more of the PAVN escaping through holes in the US net. An interesting document in this regard is *Lessons Learned, Headquarters, 1st Cavalry Division (Airmobile)*, compiled in October 1967, which collected the tactical impressions of a busy year of combat, particularly in relation to Operation *Pershing*. In the extended passage quoted below, the author reflects upon the challenge of tackling the PAVN in pre-prepared fortified villages, as was evident in the battle around Tam Quan. Two points to note on reading are the excellence of PAVN tactics in village defense and the causes of the loss of "initiative" among the US troops:

ITEM: Operations against Fortified Villages.

DISCUSSION: In discussing past operations against fortified villages, several observations should be presented.

1. In almost all villages in the Pershing AO heavy bunkers have been built that can withstand almost all forms of artillery fire with the exception of a direct hit. In many of these bunkers are hiding places under the floor boards, false walls or ceilings where personnel and equipment can be hidden.

2. In a 24–28 hour period the enemy can prepare an elaborate perimeter and positions affording him excellent cover and concealment while allowing him to defend the entire village by fire. Within the village the enemy will prepare sniper positions in palm trees or on the grounds that conceal him while he covers main approaches into and trails through the village.

3. Once contact is made and our forces encounter strong resistance, the procedure of pulling back or out of the village and calling for supporting fires causes our forces to lose the initiative and spirit of battle and permits the enemy to regroup and/or attempt an escape from the village.

4. In forming an encirclement to trap the enemy, the delay in getting elements to the area and setting up positions causes an even greater loss in the initiative of our forces. Even under artillery fire the enemy can reorganize and attempt an escape with his main force through many avenues such as hedgerows, tunnels, stream beds, paddies, or sugar cane before the encirclement can be completed. In attempting an escape, the enemy will generally leave a small covering force in the village with the mission of directing enough fire at our elements so that we will not assume a breakout maneuver.

Wounded soldiers of the 1st Air Cav wait for medevac from a hilltop along Highway 9 during the division's advance toward Khe Sanh, as part of Operation *Pegasus*. (Bettmann via Getty Images)

5. In completing an encirclement with the main enemy force trapped we have found that he will make numerous attempts at breaking out during the hours of darkness. Each sector of the encirclement will be probed with a small main force. If a break in the encirclement exists, the main enemy force will use this as an escape route and can break our trap before our lines can be adjusted. This escape route may not be a likely avenue, because the enemy can use clandestine methods to reach our lines and disappear, concealed by darkness. (US Army 1967: 55–56)

A PAVN unit photographed fighting an open battle in April 1972, during the early days of the Easter Offensive. Leaning on the strongpoint, a soldier armed with a 7.62×39mm RPD light machine gun provides cover for the infantry team, while a soldier armed with an RPG-2 antitank missile takes aim. (PHAN DUY/AFP via Getty Images)

In response to these identified problems, the report goes on to observe several solutions. From the point of view of weaponry, it found that armor support from M48 Patton main battle tanks was useful, as the vehicle's 90mm gun "will destroy bunkers when point detonation type fuse is used" (US Army 1967: 56). It also noted that the 90mm M67 recoilless rifle, when firing high-explosive antitank (HEAT) rounds, had a similar utility at company level. Other specific tactical recommendations included the following. First, villages and their perimeters needed to be searched thoroughly for hidden bunkers, tunnels, trenches, and fortifications, with engineer support to do so when necessary. Second, once contact was made with an enemy, "every effort must be attempted to maintain it, while other elements are maneuvered to destroy and/or cut off his route of escape" (US Army 1967: 56). Third, supporting fire should be concentrated on possible routes of enemy exfiltration, to prevent his escape. Finally, encirclement operations required tighter coordination between units to limit the opportunities of enemy escape: "if they are available, back-up forces platoon sized elements should be placed in positions behind the encirclement to combat break-throughs or provide rear covering forces" (US Army 1967: 56).

This sophisticated analysis perhaps shows not only the chinks in the armor of Air Cav tactics, but perhaps also those in many US military ground operations in the Vietnam War. The clock may have been ticking against the PAVN from the beginning of the battle, but by clever defensive actions and by causing US troops to rely on long-range firepower or air strikes at intermittent intervals, the enemy forces could create windows of opportunity for at least some of their number to fight another day.

Aftermath

The year 1967 was an important one in the PAVN's overall strategic model. Despite the alarming levels of casualties that the Allied forces had inflicted on the PAVN/VC since the beginning of major US combat operations in 1965, the North Vietnamese in many ways still retained the strategic initiative. The PAVN and VC could, through a ruthless logic of political rather than purely military attrition, keep chipping away at the American will to fight, especially as international public opinion was swinging against the prosecution of the war. What troubled the North Vietnamese government, and the PAVN generals, was that they had reached what was in effect a brutal stalemate. What was needed, they reasoned, was to ratchet up the pressure on the Americans through exerting military pressure on an even grander scale.

It was for this reason that North Vietnam chose to move beyond the stage of protracted guerrilla warfare and embrace a conventional military offensive, scheduled for the end of January 1968, in what today is known as the Tet Offensive. While the North Vietnamese knew they were unlikely to win a clear military victory, they hoped that this invasion of South Vietnam would provoke a popular uprising among the people (which it did not) and would cause the American people to become increasingly disillusioned with continuing the fighting (which it did).

The 1st Air Cav would play several important roles in combating the Tet Offensive. The offensive was launched on January 31, 1968, and in I CTZ the 1st Air Cav fought large-scale conventional engagements around the beleaguered cities of Quang Tri and Hue. This fight was punishing, as the Air Cav soldiers faced full-strength PAVN combat formations with supporting armor and artillery. During a single day's action, for example, on February 2–3, 2/12 Cav suffered nearly 50 percent casualties. Yet the fighting power of the 1st Air Cav played its crucial part in stopping and then destroying the enemy offensive in Quang Tri Province and around Hue. From April 1–14, the 1st, 2d, and 3d brigades of the division served as one wing

of Operation *Pegasus*, the successful mission to break through and relieve the besieged US Marines at Khe Sanh airbase (US Marine Corps units formed the other wing of the advance).

Maintaining its frenetic pace, between April 19 and mid-May, the 1st and 3d brigades conducted Operation *Delaware* in the A Shau Valley, a joint operation with the ARVN (which termed it Operation *Lam Son 719*) to wipe out a key PAVN supply route into South Vietnam from the Laotian border. A combination of bad weather and the heavy presence of PAVN antiaircraft artillery contributed to a heavy casualty rate among the 1st Air Cav, with more than 130 dead and 530 wounded by the time the operation ended.

Units of the 1st Air Cav would remain in Vietnam until August 1972, although most of the division had been withdrawn by the end of April 1971. By the time of its final departure, the division had lost 5,444 men killed in action and 26,592 wounded in action.

For the PAVN, meanwhile, the Tet Offensive was a near-terminal tactical failure. Despite a coordinated onslaught against more than 100 cities, towns, and outposts across the country, the PAVN divisions were ultimately smashed by the US and ARVN fightback. The VC nearly ceased to exist as an entity – a reality that allowed the PAVN increasingly to take over their roles – but possibly as many as 181,000 PAVN troops were killed in the fighting of 1968. It would take many years for the PAVN to recover, but recover it did, and in April 1975, the last American troops having withdrawn entirely from South Vietnam two years previously, PAVN divisions moved through Saigon as the country fell to communist control.

CH-47s and UH-1s land at LZ Stud, a staging area during Operation *Pegasus* in 1968. Total allied casualties from the relief mission were 315, including 59 killed in action, while the PAVN lost an estimated 1,300 killed in action. (Icemanwcs/Wikimedia/CC BY-SA 3.0)

UNIT ORGANIZATIONS

1st Cavalry Division (Airmobile)

The exact composition of the 1st Air Cav changed a little between 1965 and 1968, but its overarching organization was based on the following structure. The division had three brigades, into which fell its infantry battalions, which varied in number between eight and ten. The Aviation Group was the division's chief source of mobility, containing the bulk of the rotary-wing assault aviation. It had two Assault Helicopter aviation battalions, one Aviation Support Helicopter battalion, and a General Support aviation company, while its HQ and HQ Company Division Artillery had an HQ and HQ Battery, three 105mm artillery battalions, one 155mm howitzer battalion, an Aerial Rocket Battalion, and an Aviation Artillery Battery. The Division Support Command added the HQ and HQ Company Band, Ordnance Maintenance Battalion, Quartermaster Supply and Service Battalion, Transportation Aircraft Maintenance and Supply Battalion, Medical Battalion, Administrative Company, an Air Cavalry Squadron, the Engineer Combat Battalion, Signal Battalion, and Military Police Company. To this organizational model could be added all manner of attachments, including further artillery battalions and aviation companies, a military intelligence company, public information detachments, Ranger/LRRP companies, and scout dog infantry platoons.

People's Army of Vietnam

The PAVN was organized in conventional divisions, regiments, battalions, companies, platoons, and squads. It followed, in theory, a "rule of three" organizational structure, each unit being subdivided into three of the next tier of units, although operational realities resulted in many exceptions to this rule. On paper at least, a PAVN infantry division consisted of three infantry regiments, organic artillery (battalion or regimental strength), and antiaircraft, engineer, signal, and medical battalions plus a transport company to delivery logistical support. Total strength of the division was 9,600 troops, with each of the regiments having c.2,500 men. Each regiment had three battalions plus supporting signal, engineer, recoilless rifle, transport, medical, sapper, and reconnaissance companies, although the presence of such units varied distinctly between regiments. A PAVN battalion typically had a command HQ, a combat support company, three infantry companies, and separate signal, reconnaissance, and sapper platoons. A battalion might have anywhere from 300 to 600 men. Each infantry company had 60–130 men and featured a company HQ and three infantry platoons. The smallest division of the PAVN was the three-man cell.

A UH-1D of the 1st Air Cav conducts a resupply mission around the city of Hue during the heavy fighting there in February 1968. The 1st Air Cav fought to interdict PAVN supply lines toward the city. (US Army/Wikimedia/Public Domain)

BIBLIOGRAPHY

Anderson, M., M. Arsten, & H. Averch (1967). *Insurgent Organization and Operations: A Cast Study of the Viet Cong in the Delta, 1964–66.* Memorandum RM-5239-1-ISA/ARPA. Santa Monica, CA: RAND.

Dieterle, Richard (2020). "The Firefight at Dai Dong." Available at https://vnwarstories.com/vn.Firefight-DaiDong67.12.7.html (accessed January 5, 2020).

Guardia, Mike (2013). *Hal Moore: A Soldier Once ... and Always.* Havertown, PA: Casemate.

Gavin, Major General James M. (April 1964). "Cavalry, and I Don't Mean Horses!" *Harper's Magazine.*

HQ 1st Battalion, 8th Cavalry, 1st Air Cavalry Division (April 24, 1968). "After-Action Report." San Francisco, CA: HQ 1st Cavalry Division (Airmobile).

HQ 1st Cavalry Division (April 28, 1966). *Combat After Action Report, 1st Cavalry Division (Airmobile). Operation Masher 25 Jan–3 Feb, Operation White Wing 4 Feb–6 March 66.* San Francisco, CA: HQ 1st Cavalry Division (Airmobile).

HQ 1st Cavalry Division (September 10, 1966). *Operation Crazy Horse 16 May–5 June 1966: Binh Dinh Province, Republic of Vietnam.* San Francisco, CA: HQ 1st Cavalry Division (Airmobile).

HQ PACAF (September 9, 1966). *Operation Masher & White Wing 9 September 1966.* Directorate, Tactical Evaluation, CHECO Division.

Kellen, Konrad (June 1966). *A Profile of the PAVN Soldier in South Vietnam.* Memorandum RM-5013-1-ISA/ARPA. Santa Monica, CA: RAND.

Lanning, Michael Lee, and Dan Cragg (2008). *Inside the VC and the NVA: The Real Story of North Vietnam's Armed Forces.* College Station, TX: Texas A&M University Press.

McCarron, William L. (2015). "The Battle of Crazy Horse – Recollections." 25440101001, William L. McCarron Collection, The Vietnam Center and Archive, Texas Tech University.

McManus, John C. (2010). *Grunts: Inside the American Infantry Combat Experience, World War II Through Iraq.* London & New York, NY: Penguin.

Rottman, Gordon L. (2007). *Vietnam Airmobile Warfare Tactics.* Elite 154. Oxford: Osprey Publishing.

Rottman, Gordon L. (2008). *US Helicopter Pilot in Vietnam.* Warrior 128. Oxford: Osprey Publishing.

Rottman, Gordon L. (2009). *North Vietnamese Army Soldier 1958–75.* Warrior 135. Oxford: Osprey Publishing.

Rottman, Gordon L. (2011). *Vietnam Infantry Tactics.* Elite 186. Oxford: Osprey Publishing.

Tolson, John J. (1999). *Airmobility 1961–1971.* Washington, DC: Department of the Army.

US Army (November 30, 1965). *The Airmobile Division.* Washington, DC: Headquarters, Department of the Army.

US Army (October 27, 1967). *Lessons Learned, Headquarters, 1st Cavalry Division (Airmobile).* Washington, DC: Department of the Army.

US Army (May 27, 1968). *Combat After Action Report. Operation PERSHING: Battle of Tam Quan. 1st Brigade, 1st Air Cavalry Division, 6–20 December 1967.* Washington, DC: Department of the Army.

US Army (June 1, 1970). *USARV: Aviation Operational Procedures Guide.* San Francisco, CA: Department of the Army, Office of the Aviation Officer.

Air Cav soldiers engage in a firefight across an LZ, while signaling to helicopters with a smoke grenade. The M18 Smoke Grenade came in red, green, yellow, and violet smoke, and the colors used were changed frequently to prevent the PAVN/VC deducing patterns. (Bettmann via Getty Images)

INDEX

References to illustrations are shown in **bold**. References to plates are shown in bold with caption pages in brackets, e.g. **38–39**, (40).